DENNIS DELEMAR

The Wilderness

Copyright © 2018 by Dennis Delemar

All rights reserved. No part of this publication may be reproduced, stored or transmitted in any form or by any means, electronic, mechanical, photocopying, recording, scanning, or otherwise without written permission from the publisher. It is illegal to copy this book, post it to a website, or distribute it by any other means without permission.

Unless otherwise indicated, Scripture taken from © The Scriptures by Institute for Scripture Research, Copyright 2014

Printed in the United States of America

First edition

ISBN: 9781726888417

This book was professionally typeset on Reedsy.
Find out more at reedsy.com

*I want to thank my heavenly Father and His son,
Yahusha, for strength to complete this work.
To my mom, dad, grandmother Virginia, and those who helped along
the way, I love you.*

Contents

THE AUTHOR	ii
PREFACE	iv
OPEN LETTERS	1
LIFE LESSONS	36
POEMS	74
QUOTES	195
REVELATIONS	221
WARFARE	241
THE PROMISED LAND	251
Notes	254

THE AUTHOR

Dennis "Yahuchesed" Delemar was born in New Bern, North Carolina on April 24, 1985. He is the son of Denise and Gerrol Delemar. His late grandmother, Eliza Delemar, enrolled him in football at the age of four. After her death, he moved with his father to Columbia, South Carolina in 1997. From 1997 to 2004 Dennis faced extreme physical and mental abuse from his dad. Being pushed to the brinks of suicide or murder, a friend brought him a little green journal. She suggested that he write his thoughts in it to help. Dennis's pen not only helped him to cope with the pain, but his journal entries turned into poetry. Poetry turned into many spoken word performances, scripts, and a pathway to true forgiveness.

Although Dennis was a two-time All-Conference football player in high school, he was lightly recruited. In 2004, after graduating from David W. Butler, he attended Charleston Southern University. There he continued his football career with professional aspiration on his mind. He arrived at his senior year with an opportunity to start at the free safety position until March 10, 2008. That day a divine experience at the CSU's cafeteria changed his life forever. Dennis received a prophetic message from the Alahym (Elohim) through a complete stranger. Alahym said that He had something great for him to do, and it was time to walk away from football. Dennis decided to quit football along with two of his friends and charter the unknown in faith.

Months later, "Diary of Anne Frank" inspired him to start acting. He then discovered that not only could he act, but direct as well. He subsequently applied to New York Film Academy after being urged by his college professor to pursue a career in film. Accepted into the Master's program, he received a partial scholarship but wasn't able to attend. He became a self-taught writer and director in the years to come. In 2011, Dennis met Tom Priestley Jr., a veteran cinematographer. Some of Tom's Cinematography credits include Barbershop 1 & 2 and Die Hard with a Vengeance. He and Priestley teamed up on Undeserving Grace, Dennis's debut short film.

To date, he has shot three short films; Undeserving Grace, The Counterintelligent and Jericho's Rose. He also founded Yahuchesed, a lifestyle brand inspired by poetry. Dennis also holds a BS in Business from Charleston Southern University and currently lives in Southern California.

PREFACE

In the early 2000s, I can remember leaving that supply store with that little green notebook. Before that time, I can't recall writing things down. Well, at least not my innermost thoughts. I always thought writing feelings down in a journal was a sign of weakness, but Mrs. Wanda insisted that a journal could help me. She knew little, but enough to understand that I was living in hell. The hell of smiling while your insides are crying. The hell of getting beat like a grown man until blood flowed out of your nose. Reason? You got a C on your report card. Or my father was drunk and I forgot to clean that speck of dust on the countertop. Whatever it was, it created a 24/7 hell that no one could save me from. It's safe to say, pain drove me to write in that green notebook.

At first, the writings in it were macho. For a split-second, I wrote raps. I mean corny raps. Raps that were undeniable trash, and things you should never repeat throughout the duration of your lifespan. Anyway, that didn't last long. The perpetual hell intensified, and questions of suicide and revenge began to surface. In no way do I condone such things, but pain pushes you to some dark places. At that moment, I could no longer pretend. I often felt like Alahym was ignoring my cry for help. All I could do was write. It was that or do something I would regret. Those corny rhymes transformed into me pouring out my heart. For the first time, I could say everything that I couldn't speak. I thought to myself, Alahym will read my journal and have mercy on me. This was the preface of *The Wilderness*.

March 10, 2008, was the day I entered *The Wilderness*. After a divine experience in the University's cafeteria, my writing skills manifested. My writing began to develop into poetry that expressed who I was at the core. Faith grew, and I became bold enough to speak my poetry in front of crowds like my friend's wedding, to talent and poetry shows. This might not seem like incredible, but this a work of Alahym. After kindergarten, I went to K-1, a special grade for children who teachers deem 'slow'. For one, I hardly spoke, and when I did, I stuttered. Not to mention, my reading skills were not on the level it should've been. I should also add that English was the class I failed the most. So for Alahym to develop me into a writer and speaker is marvelous. Turning the least likely person into a masterpiece, so people can marvel at the Painter.

Over the years my writings turned into scripts, then a collection of all sorts of genres. This is how *The Wilderness* came about. After returning from Africa for the 5th time, (we'll talk about that later) I left a lot of my writings with someone. I was moving to Tulsa, Oklahoma to write the script for *Black Wall Street*, and could only take a few items. Long story short, that someone ended up throwing away all my writings! This is one reason for this book. Many times I said to myself, "I'm going to write a book one day." The experience of losing those writings taught me that 'one day' is not promised. We must empty the bag that contains our talents. They were entrusted to us to be a thread in the tapestry of Alahym's plan. Time is short.

Why *The Wilderness*? The Israelites spent 40 years in the wilderness for a journey that should've only taken days. Today, many people go in circles for years, never becoming whom they're created to be. This genre-bending anthology compilation will expound upon this concept. This book will explore writings in the midst of my own wanderings in the wilderness of life. Read it the same way you would view a painting. I must warn you, it's transparent and raw.

The Wilderness will inspire you to go deep within yourself to help you pass the recurring tests of life. It is my hope that it will challenge and inspire you. That you may learn from my pain, abuse, love, homelessness, faith, addictions, forgiveness and much more. May you stray no longer and enter into the land flowing with milk and honey.

NOTE:
If you haven't already noticed, you will see
a lot of Abry (Hebrew) terminology in this book.
I am of Yashra'al (Israel) and worship the
Alahym (Elohim) of Abraham,
Yashaq (Issac), and Ya'acub (Jacob).
Whose Name is:

𐤄𐤅𐤄𐤉 (YAHUAH)
and
𐤉𐤄𐤅𐤔𐤏 (YAHUSHA) Ha Mashiach (The Messiah)

OPEN LETTERS

With wonders, plagues, and power, Yashra'al left Egypt. The Mighty Hand brought them out, to bring them into a land flowing with milk and honey. After all, Alahym had promised their fathers, but entry into the land wouldn't be easy. You see, sin is a gatekeeper. It's a match. A match can burn a whole kingdom, even a whole nation. A match that caused those over 20 years old to die off and not enter Canaan. This match was the sin of lust, pride, and fear. It sparked the fire of Alahym. His burning anger against them. This match still burns down thousands of families through generational curses. It burns down communities filled with the poisons of liquor stores, abortion clinics, drugs, violence, and guns. It incinerates relationships that mirror the previous generations' brokenness. A small flame that will bring America to its knees, and torch all wicked empires in the end. Lust, pride, and fear. It kept Yashra'al wondering in the wilderness for 40 years for a relatively short journey.

These same sins kept me from internally becoming a righteous man. As you read these open letters, may it cause you to search the halls of your life to see if you are your higher self. It's critical because without being born again in the wilderness, you will die there. Yourself, your family, your community, and those at the ends of the earth need the highest version of you. Most of all, the

Creator created us to be lanterns to shine His comprehensible light.

DEAR DAD,

Before I start the letter, I want to share some confessions. Things that I've never shared and held onto for years. Lies that you may not know about. I remember, one time when I was in high school. I got fired from Food Lion and for two weeks, I faked like I was working. Every day I would leave for work and would tell you they weren't giving me enough hours. When in actuality, I got fired but was too scared to tell you, but that's no excuse for lying. Also in high school, I started running with the wrong crowd. I ended up robbing someone. We staged a robbery and did it on a Friday night. Right after we did that, we thought about stealing a car. We plotted it out, had all the metrics to it, but the plan foiled. Thank Alahym it did because that could've altered my life in a different direction. The last confession is the toughest to express. The summer of my sophomore year in college, I had enough of you. When you had the stroke around 2005, I thought it would humble you to see me as your son and not your enemy. Yet, we got into it that summer and the anger I harbored over the years reached a pinnacle. It was a summer night when you were getting on me about something. I was walking out of the house and you had the knife. When I went out the glass door, you tried to stab me, however, I shut the door just in time. All I remember is being so furious in the room later that night. During that time, I contacted Mrs. Johnson to let her know some of my thoughts. My thoughts were that I was bent on killing you. The fury built, and flashbacks of the pain bombarded my mind. I walked out of the room to do it. Right when I was walking towards you, Mrs. Johnson arrived and told me to get in the car. Alahym saved me that day from doing the unthinkable. I ask for your forgiveness for murdering you in my heart, along with these other trespasses. I've held onto these things for years.

I hope you are well at your new place, and they're treating you well. I'm doing fine, and I'm still in Tulsa, Oklahoma working on my new film entitled *Black Wall Street*. I'm writing you this letter for many reasons. After my last relationship with my ex-fiance, a lot of things surfaced within me that I didn't know existed. I wanted to help resolve them by writing to you. This letter is not an attempt to disrespect you. It's something that I would like to share, so you can see the development of my manhood for the last 14 years.

I don't know where to start, but I'll start with my mom. Looking back, there was a lot of missing information on you and my mother's background. It left me without a firm origin story. Things like, how did you and my mother meet? How did y'all fall apart? What was your plan? Did you love her? Did y'all fight and argue? How did you feel about me coming into the world? These are a few questions I have. I never got the full story. It has felt like a secret. You are free to answer some of those questions if you would like to.

Anyway, I would say growing up, me and Grandma were very close. Her passing away in 1997 really messed me up. I spent most of my youth around her and could talk with her like a parent. At her funeral, I broke down in tears. To this day, I don't know if I've ever cried so hard. Anyway, it shocked my soul, as I'm sure it did yours. Up until that time, the only real connection that I had with you was rare. Like when we talked on the phone, or when you visited. I know the times I saw you were unpleasant, and usually involved a beating. I don't remember us having a decent conversation about life or anything before the age of 12. When you came and got me from New Bern, you were a stranger to me. It was sudden, and I had no idea what to expect. All I knew was you were a the former gangster turned truck driver. I didn't know how you grew up. How was your relationship with Grandpa? How was your childhood? What about your relationships with women? What did you do in your life before I was born?

The years we lived together, from 1997 to 2004, were very tough for me. In that period, I can vividly recollect you saying almost every day, "You will never be anything in life." I lived in fear every day because the slightest mistake would spark your anger. Your drinking contributed to it as well. In the midst of those 9 years, I was angry not only at you but Alahym. I thought about taking my life many times during that period. Thank Alahym I didn't. Thoughts always crossed my mind like, "How could He let this happen? How could He let someone do this to me?" He had a plan though.

In high school, football was my talent. The few games that you came to excited me. For the most part, you were supportive. Yet, inside there was a void. The void was, I was living in fear, and overextending myself for your approval and love. Not even knowing if it was something I wanted to do, or if I was only playing so you would love me. In 2004, when I left that summer for college, the voids and memories I had would shape me. They created a bigger void that I would try to fill with anything I could.

One way it shaped me was with my self-esteem. For years, I struggled with thoughts like "I'm not good enough", "am I good enough?" and "I'll never be anything." This plagued me with depression and anxiety. I lived in fear of those questions and thought they were true. Though I left your house, I was living as if I was still there, not knowing who I was. The defining moment of these chains starting to break was in the spring of 2004. At that time, something hit me like a ton of bricks. I didn't want to play football anymore. It wasn't exciting and there was no passion in it. The great void I had resurfaced. I thought to myself, how could this be? I played football for years and it defined my life. It was the first time I wanted something for myself. That spring at Charleston Southern University, I received my life's calling. On the way to the cafeteria, I prayed within myself. "Father, if this is You putting this feeling in my heart, to quit football, then I need to hear from you verbally," I said. Then, within that same hour in the cafeteria, a woman I never met spoke the words of Alahym. He said He had something great for me to do. It was time to leave football behind. She didn't know me, so there would be no way for her to know what I was going through. It was the first time in my life where such powerful words were for me. It was a direct message from Alahym.

I want to make it clear, I don't blame you. Everything happens for a reason, and I thank you for doing and teaching me what you could. Also for being a vessel of the Most High to keep a roof over my head and food in my stomach. Recently, I've come to find out that my calling is 100% sure. The purpose for which I was born is a great one. That is to love the Creator, whose name is YAHUAH, with every fiber of my being, and to love my neighbor as myself. And with Him, share the truth through my talents, so people may be set free from mental slavery and trust in the Messiah. He is molding me into a revolutionary truth speaker, used to inspire this generation. So I want you to know that I don't hate you for planting those seeds, and I forgive you for all you did or didn't do. It's just important that this cycle is broken with me.

The next layer of how those seeds shaped me was love. Loving people and romantic relationships with women. Since high school, I've had many girlfriends and relationships with women. They're defined into two categories. Women who I dogged out, and didn't respect, and women who dogged me out, because I didn't respect myself. Let's start with the ones I dogged out. Growing up, I saw you abuse and play a lot of women. This got into my subconscious, and I did the same thing. Though I never physically abused a woman, there are other types of abuse. I suspect you either saw the same thing or wasn't taught what the right way looked like. We never talked about women. How to respect them. How to treat them like queens. I lusted after many women. Degrading them and myself. Thinking I could fill that void through sex and a relationship. It took me hurting a lot of women to finally understand. The golden rule. Treat others like you want to be treated. For me, I now desire the highest standard, so this what I must give first. Women must be respected, honored, and viewed as a gift from Alahym, not as objects.

The next category is the relationships that ended in me getting hurt because I didn't respect myself. Teaching is done by example. A man who has been taught how to love himself knows that he must be financial, emotional, and spiritually sound for his woman. I didn't get this lesson either, so it created a subconscious idea that love could be earned. Every day for 9 years I tried to win your approval and love by my effort. It was done in hopes that you would love me, yet it seemed like I fell short. This played a major role in my relationships with women. I filled this void with all types of lust. Pornography and fornication were the main ways. In my last relationship, the void fully manifested. I kept asking myself, "why does it feel like I'm always giving more love than I get back? Why do I always find myself with women who don't appreciate, honor, respect, or love me as deeply as I love them?" The answer was simple. Lust. I didn't appreciate, honor, respect and love myself. I spent years and years in broken relationships hoping they would give me what I never gave myself. Love. I've finally realized that I must appreciate, honor, respect, and love myself. Not only that, but love is a gift. It can't be earned by effort. The more you try to earn love, the more you devalue your worth.

Love is a deliberate action in which someone must choose to do. Either someone is willing to give it or not. This type of love is the one that will leave the 99 sheep for the 1, or lay down its life for someone. Love is long-suffering, kind, doesn't envy, doesn't boast, is not proud, not indecent, and is not selfish. It's not easily provoked, doesn't think or rejoice in evil, but rejoices in the truth. This love is able to be quick to listen, slow to speak, and slow to anger. A love that is able to be a great listener and translator of the heart. Hearing and understanding the truth behind someone's words. Identifying how a person needs to be loved. This type of love doesn't entertain disrespect, hate, lust, pride, and fear. This intimate love, respects itself enough to know that everyone can't be loved in the same way.

Writing this letter is the finishing touches on uprooting bad roots in my life. Roots that has caused me to bear some bad fruit in relationships. Those roots were based in lust, pride, and fear, and stem back to the origins of me. These are man's greatest enemies. They can only be defeated through YAHUSHA. He will give us the power to overcome these sins, and walk in love, humility, and faith. I know that how you were raised reflects how you raised me. Seeds manifest into fruit. I encourage you to search deep within yourself to find those seeds. We don't arrive at who we are overnight. We have to forgive others if we want Alahym to forgive us. It's healing to our souls because it will release all bitterness. It's never too late to cry out to Alahym and repent for our sins and trust in the Messiah. I love you and pray YAHUAH will prosper our relationship.

DEAR MOM,

Hope you are well since the last time we spoke. I'm enjoying Southern California. I wanted to take the time to write to you from the heart. It's been a long time since I've done that. Even though we often talk, there are things that I can write better than say.

I'll start with my childhood. I enjoyed you coming over to Grandma's house every other weekend. Those are happy memories of us going places around New Bern. I remember going over your apartment a few times. The family reunions and that basketball goal in the patio. I also remember dunking on you a couple of times. Sorry about that (laugh). Weekends were always an adventure. Thank YAHUAH for Grandma's love to always bring us together. I'm grateful for her. In retrospect, I didn't understand the every other weekend thing until later. As it was part of the visitation judgment implemented by the courts.

I do feel like I never got a firm origin story. Like, how did you and my father meet? What was the plan? How did y'all fall apart? Did you love him? What happened in your life before I was born? These are a few questions I have. You are free to share some of those things if you would like to. I apologize and ask for forgiveness for any distance you may have felt from me. Often times I didn't know how to process my upbringing. Me not living under your roof and all. This instability in my mind created a defense mechanism. It's like when a person laughs with someone but doesn't want to laugh too much. They fear being vulnerable. I know that's been me over the years. Reflecting back on it, I believe there was a subconscious thought that said, "this will be like a weekend visit, it will be over sooner or later so don't enjoy it too much." It's like I didn't want to get too attached to you. I'm glad Alahym has shine light on this. Every day He is tearing down those walls. Layers of defense that were fortified when I was a child. I understand, what tore y'all apart (you and my dad) was inevitable. I would like to say, I thank YAHUAH for you. Giving birth and loving me. Nothing I can do can repay that. I love you.

During those years with my dad, he would speak about you. He never went into details about y'all relationship. I can tell that the divorce was bitter. I would love to know more. As I got older, he did want me to talk with you more and more. I appreciate him for that. I hope you read the letter to my dad. It was tough but it all had a purpose. To pull something out of me. I'm thankful for it. Alahym used that to help mold me into the man I'm supposed to be. Now I know my purpose in life.

I want to let you know I forgive you for all. I love you and thank you for being in my life. Thank you for always telling me that you are proud of me and that you love me. It always warms my soul. I know things have been tough, but it worked out as YAHUAH planned it. I'm excited to hear what you write back.

DEAR LEGACY,

If you're reading this, it means that you were blessed to enter the world from that eternal rest I now taste. Home to the King of Kings, and the dwelling place of our heavenly Father. I have faith that as your eyes scroll these characters, that our families legacy wasn't tarnished by the many attempts to discredit the truth, love, and passion that flowed from our wells as the Creator of the cosmos said it would. The era that I lived in must seem like the stone age to you. I can't imagine what your eyes may see. Mmm. I used to try to capture a glimpse of your time. Only to shake my head in dismay. Not in dismay that there was no visual description to glaze upon. But in dismay as to how evil the world had become. So thick, so dark, that it couldn't be described. Like a heavy fog that continues to grow, even as I write.

Yet, there were many things that were written that had to take place before the end. I don't have much time to explain that, I wish I did. I don't even know if there are any scriptures on earth in your future. A future full of technology and no room for the Most High, which is crazy to even say. I'm sure Alahym is called a legend. I'm sure He's said to be a fairy tale. Surely they will mock you. Even kill you for your confession. I assure you, if I could attempt to sum up the mighty acts and descriptions of the all-powerful, all=knowing, eternally wise One who sits upon the throne. Whose name is so great, so wonderful, so splendid, so magnificent and majestic, it's defined as I AM THAT I AM. It would be an impossible task. He is The One that exists, YAHUAH.

Our Father and His Son, YAHUSHA, our conquering King who created man to share in the greatness of Alahym. Created him incorruptible, yet he became corrupted. So He Who is, was, and always will be incorruptible, YAHUSHA, had to come to earth. Yes, He touched this here earth that He created with our Father in the beginning. He came to save us from the corruption of sin and death, destroying the works of Satan. Death could not hold Him, as He rose three days and three nights later with all power and might. Our Father has highly exalted Him. Child, there are not enough pages to describe how high. There are not enough pages to describe His power. I can tell you this, that the Father loves His Son so much, that everything came into being because of Him.

Beloved, He loves you, and somewhere here in heaven's library, there is a scroll written of your life. You were born for greatness. You were born to go further than we could ever imagine. So bright that you shine in the darkest earth. So love Him with every fiber of your being, and love your fellow neighbor, even those who oppose you. It definitely won't be easy. And even if there are no books to bear witness of Him, call upon Him, and He will send you a helper, His spirit. His Ruach Ha Qdush (Set-Apart Spirit). To teach you His statues and instructions that will keep you clean in a wicked and persevere generation. I long to embrace you, to hear the great deeds He shall do through you. To also share mines, which happened when there was still faith on the earth. Until that day, do not fear, for YAHUSHA is with you even until the end. We love you. From the home of your fathers, in the name of the majestic King who shall rule from Zion, YAHUSHA, I bid you farewell.

DEAR BROTHER,

Royal princes and future kings. I hope you're elevating whether you're in the hood or the penthouse. As you know, we are at war. An invisible one at that. It's apocalyptic. Like how the Romans destroyed that great city called Yarushalayim (Jerusalem). Or how those slave ships swayed off the shores of Africa. Today, I want to go deeper than the surface, because what we're facing is far more diabolical.

Slavery never ended, it changed clothes. We inherited extreme trauma these last 400 years. We had the most prosperous and blessed dynasties in human history. Then within a snap of a finger, we are being sold for rice, sugar, and meaningless trinkets. Even to this day, it has destroyed any sense of self-worth in a country so rich. I know first hand. It's like having a college degree and having to settle for a minimum wage job. Yet, the foreigner rises higher and higher than you. Many of us didn't even graduate from high school. No money and unable to take care of our families. Somewhere broken and feeling defeated. The world tells us we must conquer all. The kingdom of darkness recruits individuals like these. They string along puppets on stages, you know, the 'good ole blacks'. So that you may vicariously live through them. At that moment, the enemy of our soul whispers, "you can have all this... just give me your soul." I don't have to tell you what happens if you take that offer. Today's social drugs seek to stimulate a yes to that whisper. The sell out has become the definition of a real man, but I'm here to tell you that it's a lie straight from the pits of hell.

Who taught us how to hate ourselves? From ancient patriarchs to riding on niggers for colors. From men who turned the world upside down to being slaves to corporate empires. We've heard the stories about the Europeans coming to Africa. They captured slaves and shipped them off across the seas. This narrative is a classic display of the power struggle that rages on in America and across the world. A power struggle that has been the elephant in the room. Victim vs. Victor. Let's start with the former. Victim, a helpless person harmed, injured, or killed as a result of a crime. The European nations are the modern day oppressors. They have committed the most barbaric crimes known to man. This narrative continues, even after Lincoln freed the slaves, we still are a victim to their power.

Not so fast. If one agrees with that last sentence, it means that you have fortified your birthright as a king and exchanged it for a peasant. If you agree that it was the strength of the Europeans that capture us, or the wits of their sheer ingenuity, why you just perpetrate their false ideology of 'white supremacy'. Does a student not pass a test because it was too hard, or they didn't study? The teacher can seek to rig the test, but there is one higher than the teacher, who controls the curriculum. The student may blame the test or even the teacher. Either way, he will be a slave of circumstance if he decides that he is a victim. This reminds me of the first man, Adam, who when confronted blamed his wife. I've done the same. This flaw was so deeply rooted in my being that it destroyed many relationships. I kept repeating the same test. Running into the same situations and women over and over. Blaming it on everything else but me. It is human nature. Yes. We can be products of our environment too, but wrong choices created the environment. On the flip side, it means that righteous choices can create a better environment. At some point, we must make righteous choices.

It's the inability to face one's self in the mirror and acknowledge the weakness. The arrogance to not surrender to Alahym and ask Him for help. These are our enemies. In order for us to be men, righteous men at that. We need to point the fingers at ourselves. We must take responsibility for ourselves first. Saying, "I let myself down. I let you down. We let us down. We let our mothers, sisters, and daughters down. Most of all, we let the Creator down." You see, Adam inherited dominion over the fish of the sea and the birds of the air and every creature that crawls upon the earth. The earth was the responsibility of Adam with the help of the Word, now look at what it has become. Sin has spread like a virus to the corners of the earth. Now the only cure is to torch it down to its roots. We are to blame for the condition of the world. The condition of our women who we haven't protected. The ones we have disrespected, neglected, and reject. Man;s poison has infected our communities and children. I have rarely seen a so-called 'African American' man call a European woman a bitch, hoe, whore, and slot with the same zeal that's said towards our sisters. It's cowardly to bully the more fragile. She is last on the agenda, and money is first. Yet, we're still behind when it comes to economics. We have put our women in a position where they must carry the load and they aren't built for that. She is a fragile and delicate flower. Growing up, I saw my Grandmother work so hard until it killed her. That same the stress and weight has either broke some of our women or pushed them towards bitterness. We must take responsibility. Responsibility says we've pushed her to be a career woman, prostitute, drug addict, and a lesbian. Beauty seduced men to lust after the women's body, but never desiring to know her mind. The definition of a real man is not to have sex with countless women. In fact, that is a weakness. Why? Insecurity and seeking validation from women is the main culprit behind this behavior.

No one on earth can validate you. Validation as a man is found the Creator. Who made us strong enough to carry the load for our family through the Messiah. We have to get our act together. We have to bring something to the table and restore our respect. Our women will respect us, once we respect ourselves. For she respects power and strength. We can set a new standard of what we love. She will follow. A woman who praises YAHUAH should be this standard. Brother, always remember, women follow our lead. We need to create a culture that has a strong disdain against not protecting our women. So if we have to take a stand against the pimps, rappers, pushers, thugs, and whore-mongers than so be it. We must protect, respect, honor, and lead our women. We can no longer treat her like an object.

What about the condition of the community? Come to any major city and it won't take long before you see that someone thought long and hard. They planned out a city map to put the oppressed in their place. So it has made us beggars. Beggars in America when we used to be kings. We are in the land of those who captured us. Do you think, if my ancestors kidnapped you, and I've benefited from your downfall, I would stop controlling you? They own the corporations and factories that provide jobs. So they can choose to employ their own. Not so with us. The lack of industry ownership in our community to create jobs for our own people has had devastating affects. If you can't get a job then create one. This way we can become not only prosperous individually but collectively. We can then think about things like mergers and acquisitions. Why compete when we can grow together? Expanding and expanding, supporting each other so we all can get ahead. A concept that is against the crab mentally. Let go of the ego, and eventually, by the mercy of Alahym, we can employ our own. Helping to get our brothers off these streets.

Bring back some dignity to our soul and race. No longer a beggar in the house of the oppressor.

Beggars who are comfortable being a prostitute. Pimped like a whore. Not long ago, I went into a swap meet in the heart of hood. It summed up the pulse of the lost tribes here in America. To my right, Hispanics sold jewelry. Around the corner, Arabs pedaled sneakers and clothes. In front of me, a nail shop, there, Asians did sister nails by the dozens. Sisters saw no problem with this, nor did the brothers. Let me tell you something. When that sister takes her money and gets her nails done by another nation, why she took a job away from that young man who is about to get gunned down. He was standing on the block trying to get money any way he could. Now we have to gather up money to bury him. If she spent that money with Tamia around the block, we can create a job in the hood, and get that young man off the block. Yet, her ignorance alone isn't at fault. For men haven't had sense enough to step up, taking responsibility and tell our women no. No, you can't get your hair or nails done by another nation for them to profit off of us. No, you will not be a traitor to our people. A traitor of the heavenly empire. Men, when are we going stand up and speak? Men, when are you going stop buying from these same companies who won't even give you a job. Take some of that money for them Jordan's, Nike's and other oppressor companies, and bring back that money to the hood to create some jobs. It is not an option. It is isn't a choice. It is a necessity. Men, we have been the reason for the shape of the community. I'm here to declare, that if you support another nation before your own flesh, then you might as well pull the trigger on your own brother, sister, children and mother. If our lives matter men, then you'll fight to put these nations out of business who pimp and laugh at us. A kingdom needs slaves to survive, but once the slaves wake up, that kingdom will fall.

These ideas aren't foreign. In Los Angeles, many ethnic groups have community ownership. They own their own and employ their own. They control and operate the economy where they live. Why, if you go into their stores they'll look at you funny. At least, these other nations have one fundamental principle. One we forgot. Love for their self and their own people. It happened during the Black Wall Street era. In the early 1900s, Negros came to Tulsa, Oklahoma. Dubbed the promised land, coloreds came to escape the bigotry of the south. It started from one building on Greenwood Avenue until it expanded into a thriving business district. We owned our own. They understood what real currency was, and it's love. At first, a lot of these Negroes had no money and minimal education, only talents. "What do you do?" Mr. Phillips said to Mr. Thomas. "Well sir, I make a fine suit. What about you Mr?" Mr. Thomas replied. "Theys say I'm a fine barber. How about I cut your hair every two weeks and ya makes me a suit?" Mr. Phillips said with a grin. Did you see that transaction? The currency was love, not pride or ego. It's the concept of saying, "let's build your house first, then you help us build mines." The Negros of Black Wall Street had Jim Crow at their back, and were descendants of slaves. They had to work together. They had no choice, but complacency since integration has made the modern Negro scared to cling to and love his own self.

But today, the dollar has become the currency, god in fact, when it's nothing but a piece of green paper. Worthless, and nothing more than a concept with invisible value. The dollar. What brothers lie for, die for, and give all their soul for. Indeed, the faces on it are like the ancestors who sold you, beat you, and hung you. Now you still dangle like strange fruit on a tree of ignorance. It's ironic how they still find a way to hang us on trees. Ignorantly worshiping the oppressor. Doesn't that sound insane? Worshiping someone who advocated hanging your mother and father from a tree. I think you forgot they had our babies fed to alligators. Or had our babies cut from our mother's womb to install fear. Only a lunatic would reverence a person like that. We have come to the point of mental insanity. Others have succumbed to hate against Europeans. In this case, you must dig two graves. We who ascribe to responsibility, choose neither, only love. Love is truth. So we don't have to take revenge. For all enemies of Alahym, whether the color of their skin, will face the same fate. He will do far more damage than we could ever inflict.

By no means, I am not ignorant of the devil's schemes and the systematic ills of those who rule. In the same city I graduated from college, a disgusting and wicked individual opened fire on men and women in the church to please his demonic appetite. I am no stranger to a European cop having his hand on his gun, while you pray you don't sneeze. It is a daily reality that 'black' men face. But what I'm talking about today is the harsh reality of how we got in this position. Cause and effect. Europeans are like a belt in the hand of Alahym. The cause was the sins of lust, pride, and fear. Spiritual treason is what I call it. Our propensity to be stiff-necked lead us to abandon the Alahym of Yashra'al (Israel) and His commandments. Once that happened, He unleashed all hell against us. He warned us.

Then across the tracks, the powers-that-be have created a hamster wheel called racism. Every time you get comfortable, they suck you right back in, to fight against a never-ending guilt complex. How can you make war against a shadow? A shadow that says, "you are mentally inferior. So what you can run and jump, you're nothing but animals." This is what bigots say. "Go ahead and protest, meanwhile we're going sit back and watch you go to prison, or slaughter yourself, so we can collect this check. Furthermore, you can point the finger at us all day long, but it's nothing you do about it because you have no power." To the uninitiated, those words open deep wounds. Words that will bring most to fury or tears. There is another way though, and we'll get to it in just a moment. I don't know about you, but I'm tired of marching, protesting, or seeing a hashtag. The end result is, all the same, we always come up short.

One of the major issues in the psyche brother, is believing the lies of the Europeans mythological status. I can remember traveling to Africa. Ghana to be exact, where a young lady there told me that to this day, a vast majority of Ghanaians view Europeans as gods. I believe that a so-called 'black' man in America and across this global have been at the back so long, that he's believed the same thing. He's believed the idols of a long hair blue-eyed European Messiah. We know that this depiction is one of the Pope's son, and doesn't reflect the true Messiah's appearance. The lost tribe male has believed that the great trailblazers in history didn't look like him, and he came from an uncivilized people. All lies. The Truth will always bring forth witnesses. For instance, dirt in Africa, the home of the garden of Eden. Dirt, which Alahym used to make Adam from, is the physical color of him. Dirt, however, is trampled on, spit on, stepped on, and treated like scum. This is a parable. We are that dirt the world stands on. We're viewed as the scum of the earth. We even view ourselves as such. What a travesty. For Alahym picked dirt to be His greatest creation to display His power. Taking a people seemly insignificant and despised, and making them a mighty nation of people. We are more than dirt.

It's time to return home. We must get to the root of our demise. Sin. Lust, pride, and fear have been our enemies for far too long. These sins should become an abomination to us. We must get free from them. Bold enough to expose and wage war against them. For the forever of our soul hinges on it. Know that the war we're engaged in is not a flesh and blood one. Therefore our priorities have to be in the right place. First, loving Alahym, the Father, and His Son YAHUSHA. Loving our neighbor as ourselves. I need you to love yourself for you to love me. How can we hate ourselves and love each other at the same time? This is the solution. The Creator's love will transform us from boys to men. He will teach us not hate ourselves. He teaches us what a real man looks like through His statutes, laws, and commandments. The is the foundation, Alahym.

After this love pierces the skin, and the spirit of YAHUAH touches the bones, resurrection occurs. Just like those dry bones in the valley or Lazarus in the grave four days. Then, you will know that we have dominion over all the tactics of the devil. We will have the strength in the Messiah to love our wives and children. It will turn our communities right side up. This love loves those who hate us. Not because we're naive, but for the simple fact that we have all been enemies of YAHUAH. Love is not about cupcakes and hugs. It is the truth in action. It doesn't excuse their crimes, nor have we forgot, but Vengeance is YAHUAH's. Revolutionary love is radical. It transforms our minds. No longer slaves to hate or being the victim. Or slaves to false European ideologies, 9 to 5's, or money. For we do not work for money, but we make it work for us. If we obey the voice of YAHUAH, there is so much in store for us. Our enemies who rise up against us will be defeated before us. They came at against us in one way and fled before us in seven ways. No man did stand against us all the days of our lives. Alahym will put the dread of us and the fear of us upon all the land where we tread, for we are not grasshoppers, the giants are! He will command the blessing upon us in our homes and in all that we put our hands to. We are blessed in the land which YAHUAH our Alahym gives us. We are a royal priesthood a set-apart Nation. All the peoples of the earth saw that we're called by the name of YAHUAH, and they were afraid of us. We honor YAHUAH with all the first fruits of all that we have. Putting Him first. We will abound only in prosperity in the produce of our business. We're blessed to be a blessing. YAHUAH opened for us His good storehouse, the heavens. To give us blessings to our family in season and out, to bless all the work of our hands. We lend to many nations but did not borrow. We don't get loans we give them. We are the head, and not the tail. Only above and are not underneath. We have been given authority over all demons on the face of the earth, even Satan himself. None of these devils traps will be effective anymore. All, if we keep YAHUAH first. Royal men we appreciate, honor, respect, care and love ourselves, we do not disrespect ourselves. There is no need for us to force someone to love us. We lay down our lives for each other if need be. Our mothers, daughters, sisters, queens, and princesses are not objects and can count on us. They are our helpers to build empires and expand families. We sow the best and we reap the best. We are no longer victims but have become victorious this day, as we completely trust and obey YAHUSHA.

It about time we will rise to positions of power on this earth. We have to think higher of YAHUAH, and what He can do through us. No longer will we settle for the back of line. We have no excuse. I press towards this mark with you, through the Messiah. Men, we must get free so our wives and children's children don't have to be slaves anymore. Let us leave a legacy worth more than earthly riches. May we look to the one who can set us free. I know you're in the fight for your life, but I need you to win! Know I love and appreciate you!

DEAR SISTER,

I wrote an open letter to my Dad expressing my thoughts and life lessons based on my experiences. After writing that letter, I thought about you. Seeing the negative fruit of an abusive and absent father within myself opened a new world of revelations. One of those revelations is that the problem extends to women too. I know a lot of you grew up without your father. Many of you had abusive fathers as well. I hope you have an open ear to hear some of these discoveries.

I used to believe having two whole and righteous parents was a luxury — not a necessity. In other words, it wasn't that important. Recently, all that changed. I know we don't decide what conditions were born into, but mature parents are a necessity for giving a child the best environment to prosper in. The soil affects a trees' development, just like how we're raised affects our character. Often times we neglect this concept. I know I did, and I know a lot of women do. We say to ourselves, "I'm fine, that doesn't include me." Yet, trying to hide behind the mask of corporate success, money, the Bible, religion, intellect, or ignorance will not cut it. The root still supports the tree. You can't ignore it. We can never hide from who we are. It will shape us into who we will become. The solution is a simple one. We must confront who we are at the root.

Throughout my observations, an absent, abusive, or neglectful father will impact a person's character. Granted, society plays a major role too, but a father who is present and whole is the answer to many of our family problems. Now let's confront the problem. I've often heard the phrase, 'the angry black woman'. It's become so much of a stereotype that it's depicted in movies, media, and print. The more you look into this theory, the more you realize it's art imitating life. Why? I call it the father effect. Where did this concept come from?

Where did the fathers go? Most people born in the 70s or 80s came into the world right in the midst of the drug era. The time right after civil rights, when the assault was on the 'black' family. In that time, the way to destroy the 'black' family was easy. It was the same formula written in the Willie Lynch letter. Devalue the man in the eyes of his woman until she has no respect for him. Until he can no longer protect her and provide for her. This will destroy his sense of self-worth, and he will do anything to regain it. This was the trap that was set, but men put ourselves in a place to be exploited. It put men and women in a place to become enemies. We gave them the power. We gave the oppressor the keys to destroy the family by dividing and conquering it.

When these fathers from the 70s and 80s had children, drugs, no work, and the lust of this world sucked them out of homes by the millions. This left a lot of single mothers to fend for themselves. Single mothers with little boys and girls. By this time, the Willie Lynch formula was in full motion. Mothers had to raise little girls up to become women with only half of the parental equation. Broken families created resentment on behalf of the mother and rightfully so. The challenge of raising a girl without any help is tremendous. Thus, this justifiable anger turned poisonous. It turned into a seed of resentment and bitterness. Deeply embedded into the subconscious through generational curses, we arrive at today. Anger can be a monster. Angry breeds wrath. Now you can understand quotes like, "nothing worse than a black woman scorn." The root of this angry was against the men who chose to follow the world instead of leading his family. That same feeling when her man saw the slave master take her children, and all we could do was look on, helpless, with no power. Similar, this bitterness is against the man who deserted them and couldn't protect or provide. This curse is based off a cause and effect model. Men's lack of responsibility and pride caused emotional instability in our mothers. Mothers who may have raised you. Men didn't step into the role of priest and shepherd, to cover the souls of his family. So she was exposed to the wolf, just like Hauuah (Eve).. On behalf of brothers who love our princesses and queens, I would like to say we hurt you. We dropped the ball and haven't been the men you need us to be. The men who we're created to be. Please forgive us. The buck stops with me and hopefully this generation.

There is a generation of men who wish to right the wrongs of our fathers. However, you must keep in mind, many men of this generation are products of those same men who left your mothers. Little boys were in that same house. Boys now trying to become men, who had to learn from trial and error. As you can see, there are not many who are stepping up to plate to take accountability for the fall of our community, but over the last few years that number has increased.

At the root of it all, one of the first solutions is forgiveness of fathers and men. Considering all the pain we caused and still cause, it's a hard task, but its much-needed. In addition, women must take responsibility too. Like we said before, a lot of that pain and anger the mother harbored, transferred to the daughter. It left a seed of unforgiveness. Forgiveness is one of those things that begins the process of healing and releases bitterness. Even if we didn't directly contribute to the problem caused by our forefathers and foremothers, it still affects us. We must be agents of change for the next person. What does forgiveness look like? Forgiveness by definition means to pardon. A pardon causes one not to take matters into their own hands and harbor emotions that are toxic. Letting men past mistakes go, holding no grudge as if your father never erred. More than likely, it's a woman in the family tree who didn't do this, so it recycled itself. Brokenness breeds brokenness. I'll show you.

  A single woman whose father left her mother, now has to struggle with the same battles her mother had. The road ends in exhaustion. She grows up secretly bitter towards her father, and in her next relationship, she brings all that bitterness. Her man, who likely had father issues too, doesn't know how to handle her anger and takes it personally. Unable to bear it, he leaves her like her father left her mother. The cycle continues. It gets even worst. The couple had a baby together and now are no longer together. Producing fertile grounds for this child to repeat the same loop. On the flip side, some babies don't even make it. Abortions are the number one killer of our people. The truth is that there are countless stories like this. It's tough to say, but most times sex is a two-way street. Another person's life can't be ended because of a persons' irresponsibility. This is a monstrous issue. The anger can also run so deep until she hates her own skin and flesh. Hate for her fellow sister, so she identifies with another race. Or hate for men in general. On occasions, the hate for men turns into an attraction for women. Trace it back, and you will likely see a man who dropped the ball and didn't pour true love into that princess.

If a tree produces bad fruit, you can pick all the fruit off, but it will grow back next season. You could wish, pray, and even think the tree away, but it's still there. Only with the Set-Apart Spirit of Alahym can this tree be uprooted. He will remove it and plant a whole new tree. The challenge is to remove these roots of bitterness by confronting the issue head-on. This is how healing occurs. The question then becomes, how is this done? That's a great question. Sometimes it's a long road to healing, but the journey is completed with one step at a time. The journey can start with a conversation with a confidante that chips away at that bitterness, and it ends in forgiveness. How about a heartfelt letter, or a series of counseling sessions. All paths should lead to a conversation with YAHUAH, who will help you become a new person. You will be reborn and renewed. This is the only way.

The next milestone is the way women view and respect men. It is a righteous father's influence in the home that teaches this. He would teach the order of the family. YAHUSHA shaped Adam to have authority over all that creepth on the earth and his wife. Not in harshness, but for her protection and provision. Alahym uses men to be the covering of his wife, thus, her submission under his covering protects her.

When Alahym first speaks of Adam, He speaks of his authority in the same breath. Adam's authority was a gift of Alahym in Barashith 1:26 (Genesis). It was a mandate of who he was, not a tool to abuse. He placed Adam in the garden and gave him dominion, and Adam learned to master his purpose in the garden. Once Adam was ready, YAHUAH brought him his helpmate to assist him in their purpose. It's interpreted that this is an analogy of Alahym's perfect will. To place a man in his life's purpose, then provide him with provisions to support himself and his coming helpmate. It allows him to be a master of his dominion, and when he is whole, approved and ready, she will be sent to him. Her support helps him in the purpose that Alahym has given them both. The man loves her like the Messiah loves the assembly. Of course, it doesn't always work out like this, and there are exceptions to the rules, but this is the goal we strive for.

In certain African cultures, you see this concept. By simple observation, you can see this in interactions between men and women. They're noticeably different from those in the western world. In those cultures, women are mostly not disrespectful to men in conduct. There is an underlying belief in the mandate of man's authority. By no means does it give grounds for a man to disrespect or abuse you, it is just an observation. If you were in the presence of a king, you would not speak to him disrespectfully. Sadly, since men have disrespected and degraded you, we lowered the standard. Though, it's never too late to raise it back up. I know it has created a sour taste in your mouth when we talk about authority and submission. How can you submit to man not even worthy of submission? You definitely shouldn't subject yourself to a man who doesn't know his role. For it will only cause chaos. We all must play our roles for this thing to work. As a man, it's tough to watch the TV, listen to the radio, or walk down the street, and then talk about this. This is another point in which we must ask for your forgiveness. Forgiveness for abusing our authority. The mandate of authority comes with responsibility. Again, your patience, prayers, and forgiveness are needed. May you find someone who embodies this, and encourages those who are on that path towards this goal.

Understanding how a man needs to be loved is the next

milestone. Love is fundamental. The type of love that will leave the 99 for the 1. This type of love, death can't even separate. It's long-suffering, kind, doesn't envy, doesn't boast, not proud, not indecent, not selfish, not easily provoked. It doesn't think or rejoice in evil but rejoices in the truth, and endures hardships. Men and women often think love is primarily based on sex. In a marriage, great sex is key, but most men won't admit that it's deeper than that. "How does my man need to be loved?" is a key question. There is no cookie cutter answer because we're all different. The love and support a woman gives to a man is priceless. One of the biggest forms of support is encouragement. Encouragement is the action of giving someone support, confidence, and hope. Seeing that our men are in a war against themselves and a world that wants to destroy them, this is extremely important. With your complete trust in YAHUSHA, and His help, all these issues will eventually be eradicated.

One more layer to go. Let's clear the air, and talk about what men really want, other than sex and peace. A unique woman. Scarce in fact. Passionate about the finer things in life that aren't physical. She is rooted in her love for Alahym, whose Name is YAHUAH. She is a silent warrior, fighting wars you never heard about. Her prayers can shake the earth. She understands her existence wasn't just to look pretty but to give life to dreams, ideas, and visions. To dynasties and empires that carry legacies that change the world. This is her. Hungry, and you can see it in her eyes. You can hear it in her voice. She pours out wisdom from the One who created her spirit. Intense yet gentle. Strong yet fragile. The balance is like a dance on an oceanfront. You are privileged to know her. Yeah. She is Ruth or better, yet she's nicknamed resilient. Failure left her vocabulary even before she could speak a word. Quitting is not her forte. She misses you when you are gone, and would pursue you to the ends of the earth. Worthy of the Creators' best prince, who will be her king. For covers her from the elements. She respects and fears him like a king. She's known in the city and blessed. Her goal is to bring out the best in him. Like a mirror. Reflecting the love of YAHUSHA. How rare is this gem? Dressed in modestly, essence, and righteousness. This is who she is to me. To us men who desire the standard of our heavenly Father. How blessed is that man to cherish her? May he protect her with his life, for surely he would give it. You are beautifully and wonderfully made. Your identity isn't in your body, hair, or looks. It's in Him who created you to be a pillar of wisdom and life upon this earth. I love you, my sister.

DEAR AMERICA,

I can hear it within the drums of my ears. The last of words of a slave to be hung, "May this country receive back double for all her crimes." And with that, his neck snapped. In the background, the flag flies high as the pledge of allegiance rings out. "Their blood has washed out their foul footsteps pollution. No refuge could save the hireling and slave from the terror of flight or the gloom of the grave, and the star-spangled banner in triumph doth wave. The land of the free and the home of the brave" penned Francis Scott Key[1]. His words feel like the spirit that says 'Make America Great Again'. America. You demonize and kill the ones who draw attention to this sick and deranged foundation. Like those free Negros that fought to free their enslaved brethren in the War of 1812. It was a trap. A paradox.

As the British enslave those lost tribes years before. Welcome to the diabolical matrix.

It's important we time travel before we can speak of this modern day nightmare you constructed. The year is 1526. When the first documented slaves from Hispaniola landed in what is now South Carolina. European barbarians grossly oppressed indigenous and 'African' peoples there. Vexed in soul, the indigenous population stormed settlers, and the enslaved Africans rebelled, escaping to take refuge. [2] This was the enmity spark on this soil. A fact that America has shrewdly omitted from its history books.

Let's hop to England in that same century. There, Queen Elizabeth rules. Her court is filled with occultist, witches, and warlocks. Names John Dee, the Queen's advisory and a conjurer of spells stand out. This small detail is a hinge on the door of the transatlantic slave trade. For people like these devilishly conspired with John Hawkins to kidnapped about 300 Africans off the coast of Sierra Leone. [3] It was Queen Elizabeth who once said that Negars are "infidels, having no understanding of Christ or his Gospel." [4] The hypocritical mindset at its finest. Manifest destiny even. For it was her who commissioned John Hawkins to transport the slaves on "The Good Ship Jesus". A 700-ton ship purchased by King Henry VIII from the Hanseatic League. [5] Elizabeth's flawed understanding and perverted 'gospel' was one meant to steal, kill, and destroy the lost tribes. Her vicious hatred against those of a darker hue would spread like wildfire. She magnified the wicked doctrine of European supremacy. Not only that, the perversion of the "gospel of Christ" became more universal. Hatred of this magnitude is not surprising, as there is nothing new under the sun. For Satan, himself is a master deceiver and imitator of the truth. From the name of

YAHUSHA being changed to Jesus. From the radical message of the good news aka 'gospel', to a perversion of the truth breeding a spirit infatuated with death, destruction, and oppression. From the chosen people of The Scriptures to people to being labeled niggers, tar babies, slaves, coons, boy, and porch monkeys. This is the pathway to America's founding.

Even now, I can hear the slave captains speak with excitement. Elated to make America great off the backs of the Hebrews (Abry). It's stated by many historians that a few million to 100 million lost tribe people died in the Middle Passage to the Americas, England, Spain, Caribbeans and elsewhere. This year, its estimated that 50 million so-called 'blacks' are in America. So imagine if a militia rounded them all up and put them into cages with no food or water. Or rounded them up and threw them into a pool of sharks. These were the lives lost all in the effort to make America great. People traded like stocks on the same block you now trade stocks. To build houses like the white house, yet justice isn't in it. To clear fields and plant agriculture in a field full of lies. After cotton picking was no longer expedient, and the sun rose on the industrial age, you discarded us with a stroke of a pen. These were the lives sacrificed on the altar of greed and gluttony. To this day, the Statue of Liberty stands tall, but she ignores what is under her feet. The blood of millions of lost tribes and indigenous peoples still cries out for vengeance.

Cries that continue to get louder and louder by the second, but they're drowned out by clinking glasses. It's the toast of the oppressors, as a lot of European Americans benefit off of the past. They say, "It doesn't have anything to do with me, plus it's in the past, let's get over it." That bigoted statement has seeped into the subconscious minds of many Europeans in powerful positions. No, we can't get over the rape, murder, and theft.

Not until you widely acknowledge, repent, and pay back what is owed.

    Please don't take this as a sympathy card, or hate speech or an indictment against all Europeans. For there are few who are genuinely sympathetic to the struggled of the oppressed. They give their best and lend a hand to right the wrongs of their forefathers. They understand that justice is an obligation of gross magnitude. These individuals know that the shoe could easily be on the other foot. It is a human rights issue that affects everyone. No, we are not talking about them today. We are talking to America, the ones with their chest puffed up who are in denial. This is a declaration of justice. The new emancipation of proclamation. Repent or face vengeance. Be in right standing with the Alahym of Abraham, Yashaq (Isaac), and Ya'cub (Jacob) or face fire and brimstone. You have touched YAHUAH's children, the lost tribes of Yashra'al (Israel). He is the Maker of the heavens and earth. He has been so merciful in allowing America to repay the descendants of those you continue to kill and enslave. America has the power to initiate justice. She can put in motion an atmosphere were the descendants of the European oppressors are obligated to right the wrongs of their fathers. For a person that benefits from injustice and hides oneself from it, is no better than the seaman who threw that Hebrew (Abry) off the ship to the sharks. By the way, no, reverse physiology will not make us feel bad about speaking the truth.

    We are aware of those tactics. Especially against the ones who fight for justice. Whether it's in America or somewhere else where we're oppressed. That guilty conscious exudes. You fear us. You fear unity. You fear retaliation. You fear losing power. Your fear is why freedom fighters have either been killed, silenced, or discredited. Afraid that a 'black man' will become a domestic terrorist. Yet, you hide the fact that the majority of terrorist are European males. Please don't forgot about the Negro Wall Street of America, where government officials orchestrated a massacre against prosperous Negros. America, you are the biggest terrorist. Whether domestic or international. This same type of fear ran through the Pharisee's veins when they heard YAHUSHA the Messiah radical message of the Kingdom of Heaven. They feared their empire would be overthrown. It eventually would be. He should be feared because He will defend us. For when the minutes of this kingdom's reign runs out, time will be up.

We are hip to the divide and conquer mind games. There's strength in numbers. Programs like the FBI's Cointelpro were created to do this. Created to prevent a strong male figure from unifying the people. Slandering them at all cost. Finding dirt on them to tarnish their character and legacy. Discrediting them in the community. I don't have to name names for you to get the picture. You discredit them to the 'good' Negros first. Then discredit them to the general European population and those sympathetic to the struggle. Public opinion influences people's minds, so you try hard to influence them through mass media. This has worked flawlessly for years, but it has rapidly lost power. There is a generation of people who can see through the smoke screen. The divide and conquer tactics like discrediting freedom fighters in the eyes of the people who stand beside them. The old Judas trick. I lay this on the table of your amnesia.

Maybe this quick flashback will jog your memory. We are aware of major corporations who discriminated against the oppressed in the early years of America. Leaving it difficult for our men to provide for their families. A direct attack on him. On top of this, America begins to ship drugs and guns from Central America and other places. Dropped off in our communities to further magnify the problem. Now that same man has a way to make money since he can't get a decent job at your corporation. At the same time, Ronald Reagan publicized a war on drugs, otherwise known as the war on our families. Just to lock up that same man, the greatest threat to you kingdom. All the while you continue to authorize imports of drugs and guns. A renewed way to break the slaves. Like how the slave owners used public torture and embarrassment to instill fear in the man. To tarnish the image of his manhood in front of his women. Now, most of our men are either in the streets, prison or dead. The women are left to raise children as a single mother. If she avoided the traps of crack and cocaine, another one awaits. The attack on the children. She struggles to make ends meet while child protective service creeps into the picture. They then tell her she neglected her child, but she had to work more than she could raise him. At the same time, educational boards received acts of Congress to further exacerbate the problem. From A.D.H.D. to special education diagnoses, it's all a hidden agenda to groom brown boys for the state prison. Until years later, the streets call him like it did his father. Results are the graveyard or the industrial prison complex. Melaninated people in this country are imprisoned 5 times the rate of whites. One in ten of our children have parents behind bars, compared with about one in 60 white kids, according to the Stanford Center on Poverty & Inequality. [6] Wait, there's more. These men who get out, can't get a job on top of already not being able to get a job. Leading him back to a life of crime or a one of poverty. Until the day he stares down the gun of a police officer who pulls the trigger because of his fear. An ancient guilt complex that extends back to the shores of Africa. A plan to wipe us out as a nation. Dear

America, it will never happen. The day will come when the Alahym of Yashra'al (Israel) will repay you double.

We have talked for years, over 400 to be exact, and it has become clear that you are hard of hearing. A nation that never had us in mind to enjoy its prosperity. I wrote this to let you know, to remember, that we pleaded with you in hope. Hope that you would not only acknowledge your crimes but repay what's owned. There was a nation who did the same thing as yours. Pharaoh refused to listen, and Mighty Power destroyed his army in the sea. The ones you oppress are descendants of those people, the lost tribes. America, please remember that there has never been a nation that has done so much evil who has escaped the universal law. The law of reaping of sowing. That law that says what goes up must come down. The last shall be first, and the first shall be last.

LIFE LESSONS

Imagine walking through two walls of seawater. Towering and intimidating, it could fall at any moment. Only the hand of Alahym stopped it. What a sight. These same Israelites, who saw this spectacle, doubted Alahym for the simplest of miracles. If He can split the sea with the breath of His nostrils, He can provide food, water, and shelter. The Messiah once said in Mattiyahu (Matthew) 6:26-27, "Look at the birds of the air: They do not sow or reap or gather into barns—and yet your Heavenly Father feeds them. Are you not much more valuable than they?" Fear had set in. The fear of change, and being thrust out of their comfort zones. The pride of thinking they knew what was best for them. They lusted for a leader and a god to help them return to their bondage. They prayed for deliverance, and once freed, wanted to return to slavery. Sounds crazy? Once you put it into modern day context, it makes sense. It's like a person wanting freedom in their mind, but holding onto things that enslave them. It's a contradiction. It's hypocritical. That was me.

I was that same person who saw the spectacles of Alahym, yet held onto lust, pride, and fear. Hoping for freedom but clinging to bondage. Lacking faith that He could deliver me. Thank YAHUAH He did. As you read these life lessons during my time in the wilderness, may it be a mirror. I pray you love what you see. If not, today is the day to run towards change. Trust not fear. Stop trusting in yourself and others, have true humility, not pride. For true humility is 100% confidence in Him and not ourselves. Not lusting after what is forbidden, but desiring what is lawful, pure, and right. This is the standard of greatness.

LUST

The Silent Sin (Rated-R)

In my youth, I can't remember anyone sitting me down and explaining relations between men and women. My introduction to it was a VHS pornography tape my grandad had. That's when the floodgates opened up to a world that no child should know about. I can say for certain, Satan seeks to recruit children as early as possible. To ingrain sin so deep inside their subconscious, until they're too far gone. Then take their life before they can repent. This is the devil's plan, but YAHUAH is greater.

Lust would be with me for the next 20 something years. In elementary, promiscuity grew and grew. For sin, there will always be opportunities, and so it was. Around the neighborhood, I found young ladies to experiment with. 1997 brought about a series of sudden changes. My grandmother died, it was one of the saddest times in my life. The house was now left with my granddad and my aunt. She was and is like a sister to me. She didn't know the things I was doing behind closed doors with her friends. I'm sure if she knew she would give me the business. Anyway, our elders used to say, "the quiet child is the sneakiest one." It's sometimes true. I'm the only child of my mother, and even though I had female cousins and aunts. I was a loner. Loners are usually all in their head and often think too much. I was good at hiding sexually illicit deeds, well at least to humans. My granddad was usually running his pool hall or hustling somewhere, so my situation was volatile because no one was raising me. This is why my dad made the decision to get me.

   My dad was strict. I didn't want to bring anyone around him, to be honest. Only girls I would talk to were at school, events, or times I got out. His strictness set the stage for college. The only conversations I had about sex was, "make sure you use a rubber son." Not to beat my dad up, but that wasn't good enough. Looking back, it's my observation that he had trouble being vulnerable. A heart-to-heart conversation was rare. Besides, relationships with women weren't his specialty either. Flat out, my dad was a player. He had different women all the time. Throughout high school, I saw them come and go. Back in my mind, I wanted to be that too. You know, have the freedom to have different women all the time. Nothing but a lie from the devil. Deep down within my soul though, I wanted love. We all want to love and be loved. The danger comes when love is not understood through the eyes of righteousness. At that moment the devil will come and pervert love with lust. Lust is tricky. It's not always an immoral sexually desire. I'll give you a prime example. Around prom time, senior year, I started talking to this chick named Gee. She and I hit it off because she was eccentric and different. Right up my ally. We weren't dating or anything but were an item. You know how that high school stuff goes. I asked her out to the prom and she said yes. To keep it real, I wanted a relationship with her. She was elusive though, and there were plenty of signs I shouldn't mess with her. That ole lust. It makes you devalue your worth because you don't know your worth. You hope someone will validate you. It's a void for acceptance and love that only the Creator can fill. Prom came and I got the suit, a sparkling green Chrysler 300, and a foolproof itinerary. Sucker. I couldn't even get her on the phone the day of the prom until the last second. Then I pulled up, and she didn't even acknowledge the car and rode with her friends. A nightmare night. The fact of the matter is, this set the tone for my relationships with women. Lusting for their attention and love just to fill a void. I would repeat this folly over and over again.

    Though I was promiscuous in my teenage years, it was in college when I lost my virginity. College opened up a new world of opportunities for me, and that was a bad thing. With this new-found freedom I had in college, I could wild out because my dad wasn't there. Playing football during this time enabled this sin. Football players had a little more 'access' to campus girls. I got involved in this little ring but not to deep. I always tried to keep a squeaky clean image. You know the type. The one who you think would never wild out. You think you know but you have no idea. After 21, I had girlfriends and many flings. To make matters worst, Charleston Southern University is a Christian school. Behind closed doors, it was far from those types of values. The thing I learned about sinning is it gets bigger and bigger. Today you steal a candy bar and next month it's a TV. It keeps building because the devil is trying to get you further and further away from Alahym. For me, the promiscuity turned into a porn addiction. It's like, once lust overcomes you, you want more and more but are never satisfied. The porn addiction was something that I would do and knew it was wrong, but couldn't stop. Throughout college, the problem compounded.

Those images I saw as a child were still embedded in my mind with the new ones of college.

One of the lowest moments of my life was in my junior year. I took lustful desires to a new level. There was this site called Black Planet, where I did my late night creeping. One night I invited a married woman over to my dorm. We slept together and after it, I felt so dirty. Leading up to it, it was a risk-taking thrill. Something I always wanted to do. Wicked. Sin is definitely risking-taking thrill because its wages is death. After she left the dorm, I got a text message. The text said, "I see you." It was one of my friends that had a dorm across the hall. When I read it my heart sunk to the floor because I felt like it was Alahym saying, "I see you", "I know what you're doing." I was shaking for days to come and was determined to do better.

The next year is when the whole football event happened, and I was talking to this church girl. I wanted to marry her, but I was caught in the friend-zone. Sidebar, if there was a reward for the most consistent relationships that were in the friend-zone, I would win. Back to the story. I wanted to express how I felt about her, so we could take it to the next stage. The day came when I gathered up enough courage to do so. I said, "I love you" and she said, "I don't love you back." It was heartbreaking. I can remember swinging at the air, wondering how could I be so stupid. It was like the twilight zone or something because it felt like high school. I told my prom date I loved her, and she said, "no you don't love me, you barely know me." The rest of the year I shutdown any relationships with women, but remained best friends with lust.

From the beginning of 2009 to 2011 I was celibate until I met Nancy. Lust again drove me into this relationship head first. The thing about this sin is, it can transform itself into something that looks like true love. Thus, I dived into this lust filled relationship believing it was love. Even making a marriage covenant with her and Alahym. A terrible decision. We were loose. I can remember the day before I got fired for my job, we went to a strip club the night before. I don't believe in coincidences. I was living a double life. Saying I'm a believer in the Word of YAHUAH, yet disobeying Him on all fronts. On top of that, I was acting like it wasn't even a big deal. Thank YAHUAH He had a plan and didn't give up on me. For "because of YAHUAH loving devotion we are not consumed, for His compassion never fail (Eyk/Lam 3:22)."

The relationship between Nancy and me was toxic. Shouting matches and physical altercations. No, I never put my hands on her, but she did put her hands on me. It was partially my fault because I continued to provoke her knowing that she's a live wire. In revenge, I called the police, and with the physical evidence on my face, they said she would go to jail. Her son would see the police take her away, and that wasn't a good look. Man. Lust can get you in some situations that are hard to get out of. I would pray and pray that things would get better but it seemed to get worst. You can't pray and ask Alahym to bless a relationship you got in on your own accord. Like one of my friends say, "He doesn't bless mess." You can't covet or lust after something, then get it and want to give it back with ease. That's exactly what I did until I came to my senses. Yet, the saga continued. I kept connecting with women who didn't appreciate or love me. I was overextending myself to be validated and tried to earn the other person's love. "What is wrong with these women?", I used to think. That's what a spirit of lust teaches you. That it's everyone's else fault except yours. The real problem was, I didn't want to look at myself in the mirror. I knew I would be disgusted at what I saw.

Once I dissolved the relationship with Nancy, it was time to move on. Over the next few years, porn consumption, coveting other men's wives, illicit relationships, and masturbation would fill my life. As I got deeper and deeper into this sin, the void got bigger and bigger. This is when you know you have an addiction. I got to a point where I would often pray "YAHUAH please take this away from me." This prayer, however, reveals the mindset of a victim. We'll talk about that in a few. Here's a prime example from my diary dated back in 2014 when I was trying to get 'clean'.

"Last night I stumbled again. Although this time it wasn't my attentions. I pray I can be stronger when it comes to sexual temptation."

If you need to get free from any type of sin that binds you, read this carefully. There are some keywords I used in this sentence. "I pray I can be stronger…" Right there. This is a similar prayer to "YAHUAH please take this away from me." Both of these display levels of pride and cowardliness. Let's start with the first. "Take it away from me", was my favorite line after I did a lustful deed. At first glance, it seems like a great prayer. Hold on. To say "take it away from me" implies that you want to escape the responsibility of dealing with it. I'll give you an example. Imagine you worked next to a co-worker who put his feet on the desk, and he said, "take this piece of trash away from me." The thing is, the trashcan is right beside him. He could easily grab it and put it in the trash. So on one side of my mouth, I was crying out for help, but the other side was unwilling to submit to the Messiah to receive real help.

It's a prayer that reminds me of a story in the Scriptures. "For a messenger was going down at a certain time into the pool and was stirring the water. Whoever stepped in first, then, after the stirring of the water, became well of whatever disease he had. And a certain man was there who had a sickness thirty-eight years." When YAHUSHA saw him lying there and knowing that he already had been a long time, He said to him, "Do you wish to become well?" The sick man answered Him, "Master, I have no man to put me into the pool when the water is stirred, but while I am coming, another steps down before me." YAHUSHA said to him, "Rise, take up your bed and walk. And immediately the man became well, and he took up his bed and was walking (Yahu/John 5:4-9)." I hope you noticed a few things. The first thing is, the man wanted to get healed because he had been waiting by the pool for a long time. The next thing is key. Notice what YAHUSHA asks him, "Do you wish to become well?" You would think it was obvious that he wanted healing, after all, he had been sick for 38 years and waited by the pool for a very long time. The question was soul-piercing. His statement seemed to say, "I know you've been here for a long time, but do you really want to be healed?" Often times He asks us the same question. I was this man who finally got to the pool, ready to be helped, yet I was still making excuses just like that man. "While I am coming, another steps down before me." Sounded like an excuse to me. "When I am try to stay focus, she made me fall." Or "while I was trying to do what's right, that feeling came over me and since I'm here now, let's go all the way." All excuses of a victim. YAHUSHA proceeds to tell him, "Rise, take up your bed and walk. And immediately the man became well, and he took up his bed and was walking." Right here, the Master, full of compassion, commanded him in authority to "take up your bed and walk." In other words, freedom from sin will only come from the power of YAHUSHA. Also, it's a two-way street, we must trust His delivering power and possess His authority to command that sin to be gone! Lust, get out of my life in the Name of YAHUSHA! More on this in the *WARFARE* chapter.

No one never taught me how to fight sin or even be delivered from it. All I grow up understanding is, the Messiah died for your sins so all you have to do if you sin is ask for forgiveness. That's only half of the story. Imagine if someone took the death plenty for you and you turned around and did the same thing that got you on death row in the first place. Also, I was trying Alahym with prayers like, "I pray I can be stronger." Why? The Word says, "I Am the Vine, you *are* the branches: He that stay in me, and I in him, he bears much fruit: for without me you can do nothing (Yahu/John 15:5)." I had it all wrong. I was trying to be stronger in my own strength. Let me let you in on something. You will never defeat sin on your own. Never. You will never beat the adversary on your own. It's impossible. You need YAHUSHA. Furthermore, suppression from sin is not the same as deliverance from it. Suppression is done by self-discipline in one's own strength. It may work for a little while, but it's like that little alligator popup game. It's still there and will manifest itself in new ways. Deliverance is complete freedom from the control of a sin and the spirit attached with it. It doesn't mean there will be no more temptations and warfare, but it means it doesn't rule over you.

After lust caused so much destruction my life and the life of others, I had enough. One thing about lust, or sin in general, is it bleeds into the rest of your life. It's a liability to everything. If you're a man or woman with a lustful spirit, no relationship will save you. No self-discipline outside of the Turah (Torah) will help. Submitting to Alahym the Father through YAHUSHA's saving power was how I got delivered from the spirit of lust. Free from porn, masturbation, whoring, coveting men's wives, coveting money and much more. Free from being so deep into lust until I invited prostitutes to my hotel back in 2014. I didn't go through with it, but it's the principle. The mercy and kindness of YAHUAH is beyond supreme. YAHUSHA set me free indeed!! He can do the same for you!

AFRICA

Lessons From Africa

It seems like a distant dream. Being blessed to touch the continent of Africa not once, not twice, but five times in 2014. To understand this life lesson, you have to understand the reason I was going to Africa in the first place. In 2012, me and Phillip connected with an individual who had business connections in Ghana. He was involved in the gold trading industry. If you don't know, Ghana has long been one of the top producers in gold. It seemed like a great opportunity. Keyword is seemed. We proceeded to do business in Ghana, and it required us to travel. This trip would shatter my 'America' taught perceptions of this little part of Africa.

Leading up to the trip, there were a lot of thoughts. The typical American ones. I know, I hate to say that. I thought a mosquito would bite me. "How many mosquitoes are out there anyway?" I thought to myself. I knew very little about Africa. Only what I saw on TV or heard. Before then, the longest trip I'd ever taken was to Hawaii when I played college football. So nothing could compare me for it. I can remember the first time landing in Ghana. It wasn't a typical airport where you get off to a tunnel. It was a tarmac and a 100-meter walk to the airport. The heat reminded me of Miami, only it felt like the sun was closer. Walking towards the airport tunnel, it felt surreal. It felt like a vertex to another dimension.

  Over the course of those five trips, there was a lot of lows and highs. One trip, my friend Zee invited me to come to his village. He lived in the country, and it was a little ride from the hotel to him. We all rode together. I enjoyed the ride because it was a chance to sightsee. Riding down their streets were interesting. I was surprised to see cars I recognized. When we arrived in the village, it was breathtaking. A village where they were self-efficient. They had their own school and everything. I had never physically seen anything like it. Walking towards the bush, a person with us wanted us to taste some Pineassion. That's pineapple and passion fruit mixed together. Let me tell you. I don't think my taste buds have ever tasted anything so rich. We continued to go deeper into the bush. You could see how fertile the land was. Unlike the states, natural fruit trees are a dime a dozen. Couldn't help but to think about the Scriptures, and how our forefathers dwelt in this rich land. Dense red soil. Fertile, like the lost tribes. We continued to travel in the midst of the bush until we came to a small river. It wasn't any legitimate way across it, but check out Ghanaian hospitality. One of the Ghanaians with us said, "get on my back." He said it with no hesitation. He didn't want me and Phillip to get wet. At the time, I was grateful but never thought about the depth of the gesture. It was a testament to the family structure that is lacking in America. There, from what I could see, family values and traditions are a stronger than the western nations. When you go to the market, you can see family businesses and many couples dressed alike. America is light years behind Ghana when it comes to this. Before experiencing this, expectations were low, but, seeing it confirmed and exceeded them.

Ghana is one of the places that defies your imagination in one area, then deepens the preconceived notions in others. For instance, entering the country. Standing in line for immigration was nerve-racking. I kept thinking about how the process would go. Then, it was my time to go to the booth. The customs agent proceeded to cross off 'Africa' on the immigration form where it said 'African American'. In my head I was "huh?!" This brings me to my next lesson. That incident may go over a typical 'black' American's head. Yet, his action reflect how some Africans view us. The majority of so-called 'blacks' in America and those involved transatlantic slave trade are descendants of the lost tribes mentioned in the Scriptures. I should mention that there are also tribes in Africa and across the world who are lost tribes, but not all 'black' people are the same. Research shows that a lot of the lost tribes were sold off the west coast of Africa by African tribes. Many of the lost tribes fled into Africa after the destruction of Yarushalayim (Jerusalem). So what he did was fitting. Many Africans view an American as an American, no matter what skin color you have. There are other stereotypes too. On a beach in Accra, I was talking with a young man who thought the so-called 'African American' males were all like the rap videos. Prideful, with a lot of money, and had all sorts of women. Also, the consensus is that Americans, in general, are arrogant jerks who are gullible. I can see that. I wouldn't say it's across the board, but America did elect Donald Trump, so the stereotype makes sense. On the flip side, the typical 'black' American believes Africans are primitive and less intelligent. I can see the primitive part, though it's not across the board.

Primitive is a good thing. I always say, if there are global famines and wars, Africa is will be the only place to survive.

Next up, the Ghana museum. Goosebumps can describe it. The chains and history of slavery. The feeling is like no other. We didn't get to make it the slave port, but the slave exhibit was powerful. Looking at the display of a small rowboat taking slaves to the main slave ship, it hit me. It was like going in a time-traveling machine. You could hear the waves, you could feel the sun. You were lost in a sense of eeriness. A feeling like something was about to happen that would shape human history forever. Something Scriptural that couldn't be stopped with the strongest prayer. The moment when my ancestors didn't know what was about to happen, but they knew they would never return. This solidified my understanding that slavery wasn't a random event in history. It wasn't by accident these people were taken to the four corners of the world. It was a divine event from the Creator. His children forsaked Him. It was written in Dabrim 28 (Deuteronomy).

Landing back in the states for the first time, and the times after that was also an experience too. Vanity. It's like there's a dimension you enter into when approaching the territory of the United States. You get this feeling like, "what is all this about? What's the point of all this?" You finally see the greed and the gluttony of America. You understand why the world hates America. How Americans have taken things for granted like water. In Accra, I saw a water truck come by to give people water like how a trash truck comes by in America. What about electricity? A few times at the hotel the power went out. It's no big deal there and a regular occurrence. But I guarantee you if that happened regularly in the states', chaos would ensue. Yet, Africa in a lot of ways is like America. In Ghana, you can be in a good neighborhood then boom, you see a little boy in a diaper in the middle of the street. You are in the hood. This is like the railroad tracks in America. Once you cross them, you have entered a war zone. There are much more similarities. In short, Ghana has been colonized. Even though it was great seeing people who looked like me on the currency, it's all a smoke screen. One day at the hotel I was reading a newspaper. The cover was talking about how an European country was giving billions of dollars to Ghana in aid. You and I know it comes with strings attached. How is it that Ghana gets all this money from European countries, yet, things like electricity are unstable? The trick is what colonizers have done for centuries. Making Africa dependent upon them while corporations rape and steal the resources of the land. Leaders are corrupt and are likely approved by western authorities. No matter what landmass you're on, oppression is universal. The difference is, Europe wants what Africa has. Africa has the power to say no, but dependence has taken them so far down the rabbit's hole, that it's impossible to escape. Looks can be deceiving.

    Speaking of which, the most important life lesson learned in Ghana was, never put your trust in man. Never ever. Don't even put trust within yourself. You can only trust Alahym. Even if he looks like you, you can't freely trust. Let's go back to our business dealings in Africa. Over the course of 2 years, we got in deeper and deeper involved in business with the Ghanaian people. The total sum of investments reached 6 figures. Promises, contracts, and guarantees. All with nothing to show for it. If you get nothing from this lesson, get this. The levels of deception in this world are far beyond your imagination. People will do anything for money, or whatever their agenda is. Being scammed by Ghanaians was a defining moment in my life. At first, the anger and disappointment were unreal. Not only that, it set in motion a domino effect. If you make a promise based upon the contingency of someone fulfilling their promise, you're in bad shape. You are close to destruction. I love how Mashal 11:15 (Proverbs) says it, "he who hates shaking his hands in a pledge is safe." Boy, wish I understood that back in 2012. When you make a pledge based off someone's else's word, you can cause harm to yourself and others. A lot of people got hurt because of my folly, because of our folly. The folly that was written on the wall many times, but lust and pride kept us going. Mashal 22:3 (Proverbs) says, "he who sees trouble and hides is safe, but the folly rushing in and is punished." This was one of the most important lessons of my life. Never let pride or lust blind you from the truth. Desire what Alahym wants for you. Never be so consumed with getting what you want until you will forsake wisdom to get it. There's so much more to the Ghana experience though, but you'll have to wait for that.

HOMELESSNESS

Without A Home

A bus, a tent, a homeless shelter, and hotels. My living quarters during the journey in the wilderness. It was like how my ancestors came out of Egypt, they dwelt in tents. What an adventure! Going through this experience, I got a taste of what it must have been like. Every day brought a new thrill and trial. You never knew what the next location would entail.

It all started back in 2012. I was working at a merchant capital firm in Miami. It was the best job I had coming out of college.

I was making like $12 dollars an hour. Not much, but I was grateful. Fall of that year was when it started to get crazy. I came into work after the weekend, and they said, "you're fired." It was a surprise to me. No warning or nothing. The reason was that I was on Facebook and the internet during work hours. I wasn't buying it. They never had any complaints against me, and I always finished my work early. That's one of the reasons I was on the computer, I finished my work and the work was elementary. What further piqued my curiosity was the work environment. Being on Facebook couldn't have been the real reason because the CEO got on the 'good ole boys' for watching porn. At the time I didn't see it, but it was an act of YAHUAH. He was pushing me into my purpose. Months before I shot my first film and was excited to get it edited. That's all I could think about at work anyway, film. It sure wasn't convenient though. I was living in Aventura, Florida at the time. Renting a room in a nice condo across from the Turnberry Golf Course. Talk about views and sunsets. Man. It was a steal. On top of this, I was in a relationship with Nancy. All this was about to come down on my head. Not soon after losing my job, I couldn't make the rent, plus the place was being sold. Then within a month Nancy and I broke up. No money usually equals no woman. So it began.

Over the course of time, my film skills continued to progress as I focused more and more on the craft. Simultaneously, my trust in YAHUAH began to grow as I had to rely on Him for my daily bread. On a deeper level, the daily Bread is the Word who sustains us with His commands. "He commanded the clouds above and opened the doors of heaven. He rained down manna for them to eat; He gave them grain from heaven (Tahil/Psalm 78:23-24)." I know this to be true. I can remember so many days like this. Needing $15 dollars for a hotel room, and YAHUAH sends someone to help. Or you were hungry and someone invited you to dinner. I can write a book on the goodness of YAHUAH alone. I saw tons of manna in the wilderness.

A couple months after losing the condo and sleeping in hotels, I got weary. I didn't understand. The easy solution to being homeless is get a job so you can get a place. Not when YAHUAH closes those doors. If you've never been through this then it will be hard to understand. Think about a force field around something you want. Every time you try to touch it you get shocked. Got the visual? You're trying to apply for jobs but something out of your control always happens. Not only that, but the harder you go against this force field the worst your life gets. Questions would run through my head like, "hold up, YAHUAH, so you don't want me to get a regular job, yet I'm struggling? I'm a man, I can take care of myself!", I thought to myself. Man. So much pride and arrogance. Thank goodness for His mercy, because we should never try Him like that. YAHUAH closing doors for employers not to hire me had everything to do with His will. He was teaching me something. Teaching me to trust in Him, and lean not to my own understanding. Not trusting in my own ability. There is nothing new under the sun. Yashra'al (Israel) had similar trials. They spoke against Alahym and against Mushah (Moses) saying, "Why have you led us up out of Egypt to die in the wilderness? There is no bread or water, and we detest this wretched food (Bamid/Num 21:5)!" Many people may think its easy to trust YAHUAH. But, when you've been a slave for so long, it's hard to make the shift. Imagine not knowing where your next meal is going to come from and its nothing you can do about it. Sums up my experience on and off during those times. I wouldn't change a thing because a valuable gem was being polished, trust.

One of the hardest things was trying to get people to understand the wilderness experience. Family and friends would say, "you should do this or that." Ha. These opinions got to the point where I wouldn't even fight them anymore, or hear them. Often times YAHUAH will show you something and hide it from the eyes of others. The purpose? I've discovered that He wants to test you to see what's in your heart. Will you believe what He says over them, the ones you love the most? Ouu.

Between 2012 and 2014 my homelessness consisted of hotel and room hopping. By that time, I was becoming comfortable with this adventure. Let's have a praise break. For two years YAHUAH provided every single day. A roof over my head in the form of a hotel or house room. It was futile grounds to focus on the Word and understand my purpose more and more. Returning from Africa in 2014, I would face another shift. Sounds crazy right? How are you traveling to Africa and your homeless? Skewed up priorities, that's how. Nevertheless, when I returned I was officially homeless. For about two weeks I lived in a bus, homeless shelter, and a tent. The bus situation actually wasn't that bad. Miami is warm so you don't have to worry about the cold. The bus was peaceful as well because it was only me. I could pray and think without any distractions. Until the police shut that down and told me if I came back I would be arrested.

I have to share this. The night the police caught me at the bus, YAHUAH was definitely with me. Two European officers saw me from a distance and did the loudspeaker thing. You know, the hostile tactics, don't move and all that jazz. They got out of the car and continued their hostility. One officer asked me, "what're your priors?" I'm like huh? "I don't have any," I said. He couldn't believe it. He decided to go on the bus to search through my things. I didn't want to show any hostility because the bus was in a ducked off area. They could have shot me and made up some story. No one would have ever known. The officer came back from the bus and couldn't even look me in the eye. He was spooked. I had to my Scriptures in my bag. He seemed embarrassed. Praise Alahym that YAHUSHA was with me that night.

With the bus situation over, the only option was a homeless shelter. A whole new world. There were people there from all walks of life. Alahym began to open my eyes. From young men who had drug issues, to men fresh out of prison. The shelter was a melting pot of those trying to get back on their feet. I don't know what it was, but the whole time I felt like a spectator in my own movie. Like these were moments that the Creator wanted me to see. Real people hurting. Seeing the people there, my worries seemed insignificant. Witnessing this stripped another layer off of my materialistic worldview. We can get so wrapped up in our bubble until we forget that its other people in the world suffering too. Suffering and in need of true nourishment found in YAHUSHA the Messiah. I took it all in. The lesson commenced and it was time to move on.

The next stop was on the bottom floor. In the midst of this homeless period, I never slept outside. One night though, it was a possibility. The night was approaching, and there was no shelter secured. An idea came to my head to ask one of my friends for a tent. She had one I could use! So that night I set it up in the park for an interesting night. Now I have to tell you about south Florida's weather. Random thunderstorms can come out of nowhere. Coming back to the tent, that's exactly what happened. It's pouring down raining and I'm running to the tent. I make it, and to my surprise, the tent is flooded. Not only was it flooded, but the storm was also blowing rain into the tent. I'm in the tent soaked, thinking to myself, "this can't be happening." Confused and angry, it felt like my life was flashing before my eyes. Those old thoughts came back, "I know I can take care of myself!" I used "I" a lot in that sentence, which was the issue. At that moment of hurt, arguably one of the lowest moments of my life, the still small voice of YAHUAH started ministering to me. "If you do not touch the bottom, how can you relate to those who are there?", He said. All this had been part of His plan. Alahym will usually build down before building up, fortifying strong roots. A tree who has gone through the wilderness will be unmovable. This person will be a walking testimony because they're not preaching religion. They're talking about the Mighty One of the universe. The One Who can do anything. The One Who they know exists because they've experienced Him outside of reading the Scriptures. This same person has overcome the world… "by the blood of the Lamb and by the word of their testimony (Haz/Rev 12:11)." I pray you reflect on your own wilderness, embrace your testimony, and share it in due season.

THE MINDSET

Abundance Mindset vs. Poverty Mindset

Have you ever asked Alahym for 'enough'? Or said things like, "I'm just trying to make it?" Words like, "I'm just trying to get by" or "I only need a little". If so, it can be a sign of the poverty mindset. You may get what you ask for. A little. According to the Word, He wants to exceed our needs. YAHUAH told Abraham in Barashith 12:2 (Genesis) that, "I will bless you… so you shall be a blessing." This Scripture reveals the character of Alahym.

He's concerned about how His blessings and miracles will affect others. How can it persuade people to put their completely trust in Him? We should start speaking like, "Bless me, so I may be a blessing. A blessing or miracle for others to trust in Your mighty power." This should be our speech. Often times the mind quacking power of YAHUAH is not experienced because we're infatuated with a personal agenda. We need overflow in all areas good to be vessels in His plan. Think about it, if your cup is not overflowing, how can you be a blessing? This goes for what is tangible and intangible. This is the wealthy mindset. His blessing on our lives is a witness. Consider your needs with the needs of others. He will then overflow your cup until you need more cups! That you may bear much fruit! Anything else is poverty and borderline selfish.

LIFE IN AMERICA

Telling Our Stories

We need more stories that unearth the skeletons of this nations' wickedness. These stories must be through the eyes of the community it affects. Why? Many so-called 'black' stories that have had an agenda. Like the subliminal messaging present in the murders of Emit Till, Malice Green, Rekia Boyd and Trayvon Martin. That agenda is in movies like The Help, Django Unchained, the Butler, 12 Years a Slave, and The Birth of a Nation have the same theme. It is a psychology warfare message that hopes to imprint a suicidal concept. The imprinting that the wicked powers can slay people of color without any justice. A concept that once digested, poisons the will of person's spirit until they feel hopeless. This is done through, racism, an invisible weapon. Deeply rooted in hatred, it's core belief says to people of color, "you're not human, your animals. This is why we can kill you like that." But who are the real animals? This idea that so-called "black" folks will never get any justice is a lie. Justice will be served for all the wickedness evil doers have done. We will not be broken by these concepts, but will remember that vengeance is YAHUAH's, He will repay. His eyes will be flaming like fire when He steps foot on this earth. Rendering justice for His people and all the oppressed. Until then, the His people shall execute punishment upon the nations with the sword of truth.

RELATIONSHIPS

Seeing Yourself

When you can see through yourself, you will be able to see through others. When you can see the ugliness in you, you can see the ugliness in others. Seeing through the representative a person sends to deceive you. They hide behind the mask of pride and shame like Adam and Hauuah (Eve) did. We all know fig leaves won't cut it. When you can see, you will say to yourself, "I know that person because that person was me." It will also create compassion to be a mirror and witness of the great work Alahym did in you.

The Mirror Effect

I'm certainly not the one to give a discourse on long-lasting relationship or marriage. I'm single. Yet, there are a couple lessons I've learned in relationships with women. The first thing is the foundation must be the Word. There are no exceptions. Complete trust in YAHUSHA and obedience to His instructions, and commandments. Second is prayer and communication. A family that prays together, stays together. Throughout my relationships, I learned this is a key principle. The very first thing the enemy will attack is the prayer life. Think about it. It's connection to the Source of Power. So it's where the war will be. A couple that understands this and is determined to fight will win. If the enemy cuts the prayer life, you can forget about it. Unless someone is willing to fight to the death, it's going get ugly quick.

    The third thing is the mirror effect. This is when Alahym uses a person to bring out the best and worst in someone. In my last relationship with my ex-fiance, I didn't know anything about this phenomenon. I took it personally. About time I figured it out it was too late. Now I know that, as a man, when you have a close and intimate relationship with a woman, who you are at the core will surface. Sometimes it will reveal layers within yourself you didn't even know existed. All the way down to the roots of childhood. There will be no way to hide it. This is a great thing. Seeing the ugliest part in you is actually beautiful. It forces you to make a decision. To change for the better, but most men are arch enemies against being vulnerable. Men who don't know how to process the mirror effect will lash out, run, or shut down. Same goes for the women. A lot of broken homes didn't have these teachings. We had to learn the hard way. Love still conquers all. A couple determined to love past hell or high water will endure until the end. Yet, I've learned that covenant love is a two-way street. If one person is not willing to love pass the mirror effect, the relationship will fall apart.

Time To Heal

Often times destruction comes when we leave one situation and run into another one. Like when a person comes goes through a breakup, then quickly jumps into another relationship. There's no time to heal. No time to forgive and learn the lessons of life. Usually, all the pain will be carried into the next relationship, creating a toxic situation. The circle continues and the wilderness rages on. The purpose of the wilderness is for us to submit to the truth. The truth is to be obeyed in faith. Faith that the Author of all Truth wants the best for us.

PURPOSE

Dear Vessel

YAHUSHA has given you a purpose to go wake up the lost sleep, so prepare for war. It's a purpose bigger than social media. It might be to go into the gutter and trenches of society, or the boardrooms of ivory towers. Traveling into the darkest corners of the earth, or into burning buildings where the so-called 'righteous' are to clean to go. We must roll up our sleeves and get dirty, fishing for men with wisdom. Remember, YAHUSHA said, "It is not the healthy who need a doctor, but the sick (Matt 9:12)." So focus on the ones you're sent to!

Imagination

One day, YAHUAH allowed me to see something that perplexed me. A child got off a school bus, and in an unidentifiable joy, he ran down the street as if he were flying, arms stretched. He thought he was a bird. I thought to myself, "where did this sheer excitement for life go when we got older?" You would never see an adult do this, if you did, you would think he's crazy. That is a parable of how people look at others, who have an imagination even though they're an adult. Alahym gave us an imagination for a reason. On this vicious journey called life, someone convinced us that our imagination wouldn't get us anywhere. That's a lie. The universe contains the creativity and imagination of YAHUAH! The real question is; If you do not have an imagination, are you crazy? Can you see the imagination of YAHUAH when you walk outside, or has life kidnapped the child in you?

Character and Purpose

I believe your talents are sync with who you are as a person. True progression to your high calling in life is not found in "honing your craft or talent", but in "honing your character". As your character progresses, so will your talent. Let Alahym build down and solidify your foundation. Forsake consuming thoughts of; How high will the building be? If you want the best, become with best within yourself, only with the help of the Messiah.

Bigger Level, Bigger Devil

The bigger level, the bigger devil in the matrix. The higher you go, the more that Alahym will require of you. On earth, as you rise in evaluation from the ground, the less you can breathe. If you keep rising, oxygen will be so scarce until you can't breathe on your own. Trust. The higher you go in Alahym, He says, "there is more that I require of you, come higher!" The less you can rely on your own understanding, logic, and assumptions. You must rely on His Set-Apart Spirit. Stay tucked away under His wings. At some elevations, it will only take you breathing one time on your own, and you die. It will only take one time leaning to your own understanding and your dead. You may cost other people their lives too. So be sure to count the cost before you ask YAHUAH to take you higher. Are you sure you want to go to war? Are you ready to lay down your life if need be? For it will cost you something.

The Caterpillar

YAHUAH will sometimes do to you what He does to the caterpillar. To you, it looks like you're trapped. You keep praying for a way out of the cocoon. The process. Sometimes asking for a swift salvation swoop can go against His will. If He hurried up and saved you, your wings would not be strong enough to fly to the heights He desires for you to go. Once your wings are strong enough, your cocoon and current circumstances will no longer be able to hold you. He will give you a new measure of His Ruach Ha Qdush (Spirit) to bust out and be unstoppable in Him. At that point, you will know Him in experience. "Not by might nor by power, but by My Spirit," says YAHUAH of Hosts (Zach 4:6)." So while in the cocoon, pray He will strengthen your wings to fly to the heights He desires. For this process only comes around once.

FAITH

Make The Jump

Alahym will often not give you all the details up front. It would seem as if He only gives enough information for you to get you to a certain spot in your life. The whole time His plan is much bigger than what you think. A little faith to complete trust. These incremental test of obedience prepares you for higher levels of obedience. So make the jump.

What Is Faith?

The word faith has become synonymous with belief, and belief is vague. You can believe in good or evil. You can believe that aliens from outer space made mankind. The possibilities of believing in ideas are endless. Believing by English standards is 'acknowledging that something exists'. A person can believe in love, but not practice it. One can believe in mercy, but not give it. People claim they have faith in Alahym, yet they don't obey His voice and instructions. I know about that one. This is how the true meaning of faith got perverted. To understand the original context of the word we must go to the language it was written in. There are a couple words that connect to faith. First up, amunah. Amunah is not knowing something exist, but being firm, rooted, and unshakable. The root of amunah is aman. Aman was a common way to end prayers. It means to be established, assured, trusting, reliable, stand still, and verified. Think about a tree. I never saw a tree get up and walk anywhere. It is secure in the ground. This ground is metaphorically YAHUSHA. "He commanded them, saying, "Do this in the fear of YAHUAH, faithfulness (amunah) and with a perfect heart (2 Dabra/Chron 19:9)."

Combine this word with batch. Batch means to trust, have confidence, be bold, secure, feel safe, and careless. "Blessed is the man who trusts (trust) in YAHUAH, whose trust is YAHUAH. His delight is in the Turah (Torah) of YAHUAH, and on His Turah (Torah) he meditates day and night. "For he shall be like a tree planted by the waters, which spreads out its roots by the river, and does not see when heat comes. And his leaf shall be green, and in the year of drought he is not anxious, nor does he cease from yielding fruit. Trust (batch) in YAHUAH with all your heart And do not lean on your own understanding (Tahill/Psalms 1:2, Yara/Jerem 17:7-8, Tahill/Psalms 3:5)."

Now let's bring these two words together. A person who really has faith, trusts (batch) the foundation it's planted on, therefore, he will be immovable and secure (amunah). Two words that are game changers and clears the smoke of confusion. When you are firmly rooted, you don't trust in your job, money, people, or even yourself. You trust in the Rock, the Foundation, the Word. This truth distinguishes people who have completely surrendered their lives to the Messiah, from those who have this faith (believing He exists) in Him. Amunah and batch are like when Abraham was about to sacrifice his son. Like when Daud (David) was secure enough in YAHUAH to let Goliath know that he would have his head. The Disciples walked in Amunah when they dropped everything and followed the Master. This is true faith. Trust and security. Are you willing to drop everything for the Kingdom of YAHUAH? Even its family, friends, or a job?

THANKFULNESS

The Thanksgiving Jar

Thankfulness breeds a joyful heart. During this journey, I got so consumed with the future. Goal setting, dreams, hopes, and aspirations. Nothing is wrong with those things. Actually, they are great to do, but if not checked, it will consume you with worry. You're always looking for a goal to be completed. You're always praying for the next thing and the next thing. Seems like spiritual gluttony. I know all about this. I was always consumed by the future, then when He answered me, I forgot all about it what He did. Almost like a baby. You know when a baby wants a toy because someone else was playing with it. Then when they get it, they play with it for a minute then they're on to the next toy. It's funny, but that was me and it could be you.

One day the Most High sent someone to sow an idea into my life that radically shifted my gratitude meter. They talked about putting answered prayers and the awesome deeds of YAHUAH into a jar. Writing on small pieces of paper, letting them build and build. From my experience, it does a number of things. One, it makes you more attentive to the Hand of YAHUAH in your life. It forces you to pay attention. It's so many miracles we've missed on the daily bases because the next shiny toy consumed us. Next, it breeds a mind of thanksgiving. Every so often you can take things out of the jar and have a praise party. Praise YAHUAH for all the great things He did that you may have forgotten about. Imagine if Yashra'al (Israel) did this in the wilderness. They wouldn't have been complaining and grumbling that's for sure. This exercise helps eliminate those attitudes. The final way it helps is this, your mind can exist in the past, present, and future.

Your thankful for what Alahym has done in the past. You enjoy the day to day present, and you're excited what He will do in the future. That's what you call, a cup running over. This exercise takes effort, but the day when you're feeling down, or feeling like He hasn't blessed, get your jar. "I will bless YAHUAH at all times, His praise will continue to be in my mouth. Rejoice I say, again I say rejoice (Tahill/Psalms 34:1, Phil 4:4)!"

LOVE FOR SELF

The Golden Rule

Such an easy concept yet it's so complex. Complex enough that people go their whole life and never get it. One sentence. Love your neighbor as you love yourself. It took me a long time to understand it. I thought I had it. This is one of those parables that you assume you know what it means, but when have you sat down and thought about it? What does that mean? I would read this and be like "yeah, I do that. It's simple." Not quite. It's the biggest assumptions of all. We all assume we love ourselves! I remember Alahym showed me one day that I didn't love myself. I felt embarrassed. See, if you hate yourself, how can love someone else? How can you know what the standard of love is? There are people who use and abuse people and call it love. I'm guilty of that. So one can say, "I do love you as I love myself," only their definition of love is hate. They may not know what loving themselves looks like. I'm not talking about anything conceited. True love. In the wilderness, I learned what loving yourself looks like. First, the definition of love must be unpacked. In short, from a Abry (Hebrew) point of view, love is called ahaba. Ahaba in Abry (Hebrew) means "to give." Let's do some mathematics. Ahab (love) means to give. So to ahaba (love) yourself means to give yourself something?

Give yourself what? I'll tell you. YAHUAH made me a kind person. It's in my DNA, but even though that's cool, it can be a liability. YAHUAH pulled me aside sort of speak, and revealed to me my error. I was giving to people, from time to whatever, but it wasn't fulfilling the commandment. Why? The motive and perspective. Let me give you a parable. Imagine you had a family, and your family was in poverty. Yet, as a man, you went out of your way to help another family when your own family needed that provision. It seemed noble, but look again. Sha'ul wrote in 1 Timo 5:8, "Now if anyone does not provide for his own, and especially *his* household, he has denied the faith and is worse than an unbeliever." A man's family is like his own flesh. As a man, preparation for a family starts with loving YAHUAH and your neighbor as yourself. Broken down even further, you are the person you're with the most. You're everywhere you go. Once again, to ahaba is 'to give something', but what is it? Your best. Give yourself what the Word says about ahaba. Be patient, kind, not envying, not boasting, not proud, or dishonoring yourself. You're not self-seeking, or easily angered, or keep records of wrongs against yourself. You don't delight in evil but rejoice in the truth within yourself.

Ahaba is about giving devotion and time too. Have you ever been so busy helping everyone else yet your cup is empty? It's not noble. If we can't give ahaba to ourselves, you can't give it to others because you won't have any to give. We are simply cups. Everyday, Alahym rains down His love upon us. We bask and recycle it into our soul. Then, with an overflowing cup, we ahaba others. Look at the body of the Messiah. A brother or sister is part of the body. "Everyone who hates his brother is a murderer, and you know that eternal life does not reside in a murderer (1 Yahu/John 3:15)." See, if we hate our own body we are murderers! Thank goodness YAHUAH showed us what ahaba is. "We love Him because He first loved us. For Alahym so loved the world that He gave His one and only Son, that everyone who believes in Him shall not perish but have eternal life (1 Yahu/John 4:19. Yahu/John 3:16)." The Father "gave" us His best. His son. This is standard, the best ahaba.

I challenge you to speak the Shama (Dabar/Deut 6:4-5) every day as we are commanded. That you love YAHUAH will all your heart, soul and strength. I challenge you to affirm to yourself every day that you ahaba your neighbor as yourself. Speaking words of life to yourself. Words like, "I appreciate, honor, respect, care, and love (ahaba "give to") myself and others." Find words of life that work for you. Loving your neighbor as yourself isn't as simple as you thought huh?

LIFESTYLE

Materialism Vs. Freedom

The wilderness journey is fertile ground for creating a lifestyle that is joyful. A lifestyle that is whole, successful, and living life on purpose. This is different from what America teaches its students. According to the World Health Organization, the United States is the third most depressed country in the world. [7] Yet, the American middle class makes more money in the world compared to any other middle class. I'm convinced one source of this widespread depression is unfulfilled lives. Lives that have accepted the materialist worldview. In comparison, recent neurological research has shown that people who get the most purpose out of life are the ones who serve in the form of giving.[8] It makes sense. Ahaba (love) means 'to give'. The Scriptures have always talked about this and now science is catching up. We're designed to serve and share our talents from a place of passion that exists deep within us. YAHUAH put everyone on this planet for a reason. To find that purpose, we must dig deep within the Word, and dig within ourselves. Finding gold takes effort.

    I went to college and got a four-year degree. Looking back, I would say college is more of an experience than preparation for the real world. Though I'm not against certain types of education, it's time we change our viewpoint on it. Take Derrick Wayne for instance. Bills, dinner, shopping, trips, broke, payday, repeat. This is the lifestyle of Wayne, a twenty-five-year-old with a Bachelor degree and massive debt. The clock is ticking on his student loans and college didn't serve him well. He thought his degree would carry more weight in the job sector. "Sorry. You don't have experience," is a phrase he's heard often. The only option is the corporate ladder. There, he needs to put some skin in the game, to get experience, and experience leads to a stronger resume. He can then apply for a better position. He needs a better job, which equals more money to pay for bills he's struggling with. If he gets this next job, he'll be happy and have a better lifestyle. So he thinks. This is a common story all throughout America. It leads to thousands of people either losing their minds or taking their lives. Depression is a monster. It's time to create a new lifestyle.

    Lifestyles are expressed in both work and leisure behavior patterns. These patterns include activities, attitudes, interests, opinions, values, and allocation of income. It also reflects people's self-image. In other words, the way someone sees themselves and believe how they're seen by others. Lifestyle is melting pot of motivations, needs, and wants. It's influenced by factors such as culture, family, and social classes. [9] See how complex a lifestyle can be? So many things can influence a person day to day.

The modern day concept of a lifestyle has been synonymous with a materialistic worldview. What is a materialistic worldview? I'm glad you asked. It's a worldview that states that material success is the highest value in life. Material success is thought to be a gateway to personal joy, improved health, and a great life. This doctrine is prevalent in western society. As stated before, the United States is one of the most depressed countries in the world. Yet, the American middle class makes more money in the world compared to any other middle class. America exudes a perpetual obsession for obtaining money, goods, and status. The goal is to fulfill human voids. The statistics tell another story. It tells us that with the simple addition, we can conclude that the materialistic worldview is a vain one. Getting rich, famous, or having all material things you want will not bring true joy. It is superficial. Humans must view a righteous lifestyle through the eyes of the original man, Adam. He received instructions from YAHUAH to keep. These instructions would be the key to a fruitful and prosperous life filled with milk and honey. As we know, he didn't follow those instructions and like many people don't today. There is no way to find true joy and passion without The One who created such a thing. Experiencing the depths of His character will reveal who we're meant to be. A person full of love, joy, peace, patience, kindness, goodness, faithfulness, gentleness, and self-control. This is the lifestyle we should all seek. The lifestyle of eternity and heaven.

I hope you dig within the layers of Him to reach that treasure. Then, you will know how to dig within yourself.

MONEY

Money Is An Idea

Money is neutral. In fact it's worthless. It's a piece of paper that someone attached value to. Money is an idea. A mere proxy or tool if you will. Ideas are elusive. This is why people who chase money never catch enough of it. We must get free from the idea of money. A concept that we must put it in its place. An object not worshiped. I know this sounds backwards from society. The Word says, "seek first the Kingdom of Alahym and His righteousness, and all these things will be added unto you (Matt 6:33)." Therefore, we don't worry about an idea. Neither does this idea worry us. For we seek what is not of this world. An everlasting state of being in which the idea of money is not even relevant. So let's start now. Granted, the world markets run off money, but it should not control us. It should not control our lives because at that put it has become a god. Money is an idea that should serve us in the purpose that is found YAHUAH. I've learned that once you're no longer a slave to an idea, it will then chase you. You ever overexerted yourself for something, only for it to elude you? Then when you began to focus on what was pure, boom, the things you needed showed up right. This is a universal law of sowing and reaping. When you become free from things, you can be entrusted with it. Money on this earth is only a tool, until it's wiped out as a currency.

THE TRUTH

Lies Uncovered

I can remember playing football ever since I was four years old. The New Bern Bears was my first team. At four years old, I couldn't even play because I was too young. They made me the water boy until I was five. For roughly 18 years I excelled in the sport. At Charleston Southern University, my eyes were on the NFL or CFL. All until my senior season. Spring of 2008, I went on a missions trip during spring break. That's when things started the shift. A couple of years ago, I was in Miami partying it up for spring break, so this was a major change. During the trip, I started to bond with Daniel and Eli. We all played football together and hung out here and there. Something special began to brew. Returning from the trip, the buzz started to build about spring football. For me, it was going be the first time I was going to start at my position. I fought throughout my college career to put myself into starting position. I felt with my size and speed, all I needed was a breakout season. There was only one thing in my way. I began to have this weird feeling in my gut about football. Like, I didn't want to play anymore. "What am I doing?", I thought. This feeling came out of nowhere, so I thought.

Before spring break, I was pumped about the season, but within a week, something changed. One day after spring break, I was walking into the cafeteria and saw Eli. I said something like, "I don't know about football anymore." Funny thing was, he felt the same way. Later to find out, Daniel felt it as well. Very strange we thought, but being spiritual, we started praying. The first meeting for spring football was approaching. So we prayed and prayed with no sure answer. The day came when it was the first meeting for the season. That morning I prayed within myself, that if this was the Father, then I needed Him to speak. We entered the cafeteria, and within the hour, a lady I never met caught my eye. For some reason, I felt like we should talk to her. We did. Then, it was like the Messiah took control of her mouth. She began to say things that only He knows and told us that now was the time. The door was open. The vote was unanimous and my prayer was answered in a mighty way. We quit football that day. The whole experience was a dream, and it caused an uproar. Eli was to be the starting quarterback. I was the starting free-safety and Daniel had a major position too. Word spread to the news media and a story was done about it by the local ABC station. *From the Field to the Soul Field* was the name of the story. They interviewed us about the decision. One of the first lessons I learned during this transition was, you never know who is with you until you take a stand for what you believe in. I lost many relationships from that decision. Most of them thought I was crazy. I remember, even the Athletic Director said to us, "don't tell anyone God told you to walk away from football. He doesn't do stuff like that." Keep in mind, this was a Christian school.

Three months later, Eli, Daniel and I were still trying to figure out what was the next move. We walked away from football, now what? I got into acting and directing after seeing *Diary of Anne Frank*. I also started taking spoken word more serious and began performing. I unknowingly had a talent of directing too and took some summer classes. Someday in June 2008, I was sitting in the apartment with my pen and pad about to write a poem then boom! This beam of inspiration hit me in the head. It was the title of a movie with all the characters and everything. I didn't know it was a movie until later. Originally, I thought it was a stage play, but it was a movie. A detail I want you to remember. Before graduation, I applied and was accepted to the prestigious New York Film Academy. I was so happy, but the $100k price tag ended that excitement. They were only giving me about $10k. We tried to get loans and nothing worked. All my plans at that point fell apart. My only option was to get a regular job and live with my grandmother. I tell you, it was blown to the chest because for a little while I felt like a failure. Then I couldn't even get a decent job being a college graduate! That's when all I could do was write.

Remember that movie idea of 2008? At my grandmother's house, it turned into a script that I worked on every day (haven't produce this movie). There's a character in the story who is very deceitful. He does something in the movie that is so diabolical that he sets in motion a domino effect that would spread like a virus. One day, I was thinking about him, and working on this story, and I heard a still small voice say "Constantine." In my head, I was like, "what about him?" Curious, I looked him up. The first thing that popped up was 'March 7th, 321 A.D. Constantine made the first law to change to sabbath to Sunday'. My jaw seemed to drop. He was like the character in the movie, only this was real life! This piece of information shattered my world. I had been deceived all those years. I begin to pray and seek Alahym more. Little did I know the Sabbath was only the tip of the iceberg. This life lesson stripped me of what I thought I knew. Just because everyone is going in one direction, doesn't mean its the right way. Praise be to YAHUAH for removing the veil off of my eyes!

POEMS

Can you picture it? The sea closing, and inside it is all the bondage of Egypt. The song of Mushah (Moses) begins to ring out. A ballad verbalizing the power and strength of Alahym, who crushed His enemies. Miriam the prophetess takes a timbrel as all the women follow her lead with dancing and joy. It's poetic. He planned every line of this story. From a baby boy being put into a basket and send down the Nile river. To the Yashra'al (Israel) being so desperate until all they could do was cry out. Before one tear fell, the solution was already scripted just so Yashra'al (Israel) could meet and worship the Creator. Worshiping Him in freedom and obedience. A Creator who seemed mysteriously silent for centuries. His plan was poetry. Delete a single line and the rest of the story doesn't work. Sounds a lot like my life.

For years, I shook my fist at Alahym. "If you love me, why do You allow this to happen?!", I said in my pride and confusion. How could He let me be abused for years with no one to help? How could He let me be broke and always be last, the tail, the outcast? What about being homeless Or wondering how I was going to survive the night? The list goes on. The things I would say to Him, He could have struck me down. Thank goodness for His forgiveness and loving-kindness. Let me tell you, slavery, whether physical or mental, can bring out the worst in you. It's poetry in motion. You can't skip a letter or a word.

Years after March 10, 2008, in a park in New Bern, North Carolina, the answers came. During the meltdown, and in tears, one of the clearest revelations pierced my soul. He allowed me to go through hate, to know what it is to be loved. He allowed me to be homeless, to know that my home is in Him. He allowed me to be poor, to know what real wealth is. How can you testify about something you haven't experienced? He impressed upon me. My life has been a poem. As you read these poems, take your time. Line by line, let the words marinate. May these words inspire you to know that as long as you stay in YAHUAH's hands, not one line will be out of place.

Shake of The Dust

Rise in the eyes of greatness
For you were born for it
You were built for it
Bricks of struggles lay the foundation for
The feeling
The moment
The victory
The chapter
The sentence
In this story
When tears fall
Watering thoughts of the pass
When the fight seemed like it would never stop
When stopping crossed your mind
Then you remember that those moments

Couldn't compare to this joy
That you now hug with a tight embrace
Streams down your face
Which are recycled tears
For you sowed many
And to your surprise
He remembered every single one
Just so you could see them again
In this moment
In this chapter
In this sentence
That only had one word to express it
It said
Mmmm

Summer Drought

Drylands
Summer drought
Has caused the farmer to route
His prayers to the clouds
What's the use?
By the sweat of the brow
As these grounds echo loud
The hurt
In a desert oasis of silence
I was told it would rain over and over
The violence of the sun's rays make me no longer sober
Beating progress, withering growth
The farmer had enough seeds to plant
But didn't calculate the rain

The pain those roots must feel
Melting in this summer heat, damaged
From a distanced vantage, the image is clear
How could the roots trust pedals?
That touch the soil of broken words
Missing its vibrant colors of expression
The love of its pedals affection
A farmer's daydream
But streams of teardrops
Are not enough to water deep roots
So its as if, it's as if
He will watch the crop die
Broken pieces, so what's the use?
What's the use of a harvest that still needs life
Like it was air
A share of joy not invisible these days
While the sower weeps over his seeds
Remembering joy comes in the morning
So what's the use?
Oh neglected roots
It's not that the farmer forgot or cared less
With careless timing, summer drought
The roots and farmer need each other
An undeniable fact
But a lack of rain has made days seem like years
Summer drought
With a verbal route
Towards what holds the condensation
Hoping it will give the roots confirmation
That the drought is over
With showers from the heavens

Mending the soils broken pieces
But the thesis of this farmer's objective was faulty
Lofty in fact, because he planted on the wrong soil

Distance

Distance gaps are but a fraction in a 24-hour day
Yet precious time is measured in intervals of power
Our smile's electricity will close that space
Until we're face to face
At least in my mind that is

Freedom Ain't Far

Looking out the window
I saw a scene that would bring any being low
Allow me to let this plane flow
Through your clouds.
I know what you're thinking
But this isn't your ordinary flight
On the contrary, it's from sunset to sunset
On the last days known to man.
Things develop like the coldest summer
Similar to how our color is said to be out of place.
Laced with the dreams of the enemy in our head
It started when the edict couldn't be read.
Shipped off on Atlantic tops
The nightmare didn't stop.
Sold and whipped
Lynched and soul beat.
Sinking sand were those lashing

Embedded in the psyche.
Fast forward there's a sudden lighting, flash, crack, boom
"Don't assume that's the door!"
I screamed.
I've seen this part before
The ominous open, to a bottomless floor.
We step, up out of chains
But the pain of bondage is still felt
Civil rights melt integration
But as Martin was pacing
He had an unshakable thought.
All that we fought for, was just a trap door.
As this flight soars in the heavens, I adjust my seat.
I think, how can we beat the odds on every corner?
Whorehouses promising us some sort exit
So I look back out the window to see if we could make it.
There, they were in the middle of a game
The kind were if you can push the rock
You can earn stock
But it shares leave you locked and chained
I'm talking about on brains.
A 400-year rink
Circles of a hamster in a wheel
Yet, I see a war General in the back.
Tattered, but stands with a royal vibe
Like He survived the darkest death.
Now at rest with future implications
No matter the visual complications being played out.
"Game set!"
The referee says, and just before he says match
The General lights a match and says

"everyone better run!"
Then states that, "He is the Son
And the universe rotates around His very vocal cords"
The locals jet for the door
I'm now on the edge of my seat
As I anticipate more.
He says, "the room has but four seconds to clear"
But some stand with no fear
Like they couldn't hear
But they shoulda took heed.
The fury in His eyes. said it all
A flame so hot it would melt layers upon layers of mercy
I'm talking an inferno
Like none I've ever witnessed before.
And with that forward
He torched the place down to the roots.
I'm mean down to the reeds
In the ocean where
Where they thought they were going to hide.
It blow my mind.
Sitting back in this seat
I thought to myself
Babylon lied.
Cause even though our sin brought captivity upon our heads
The floor will be filled with crimson reds.
So, may we exit her bowls
Cause we living on the edge.

A Thank You Note

I wanted to make a poem that you could groove to

If you do that type of thing
Not a one night fling
Cause this dance lasts forever
Clever tones and sweet bridges of joy
More than the news that it's a boy
From one end to the other
A blue note sway
Like… like
Smiles at the beginning of the day
Just for rising
Just for flying
Just for dying
To-self
Then being able to pen this
It's a miracle
One of those thank you cards
Often not scribed
In need of nothing
It's miles long too
Meters deep
High as it can reach
In fact, give me your cup
Sup and drink
A joy not predicate off of circumstances
Nor shaken by it
That's that just because joy
Thankfulness and gratitude
From the Source
Bookmark that on your upper chrome

Already There

Already there
Where the plane of trust has taken me
Past the time zone of now
Somehow we boarded
A private jet that flies international
Through ancient customs and borders of the impossible
Ain't no stopping us now

Faith

Feathers of a nomadic bird
Grabbing wind at every turn
Trusting the invisible to keep it afloat
Like saving
Words that calm storms
From a boat
Unseen yet it's matter
Factor in its elements and properties
The Word's real estate covers everything that exists
The risk of flying only gets complicated
When your eyes leave you grounded
Because freedom can't be seen
It can only be felt

Blood of Slave

Fasten your fiber optical seat belts
As we travel through this atmospheric pressure.
Blood of slave, heart of a king

I said let freedom ring, let it ring
From incarcerated minds frozen in time
Just like blind minds stuck in 1849.
Oppressed, stresses, corroborated with death
But it was only a test.
Pressed into a bottomless pit
Fitted tight across the Atlantic
Frantic, we panicked.
Less of a man I now feel
Stuck in this Babylonian time reel.
No airbags to cushion us for this fate
So we become lactose intolerant
To the freedom state of mind
With no vertebra in our spins.
We have lost our balance
Immune to freedom
So free him… My brother.
My brother
Why are you fooling yourself?
Ancestors gave us a new avenue for better health
But the extermination of our minds binds our greatness
While Caesar takes us
Behind these steel pyramids and great monuments
Creating a revolving door
With nothing else in store but death and deceit.
Rewinding cultural, you adulterer.
Lying in bed with defeat, who has painted a portrait
And we remain stuck in the frame of mind
Forgetting about of forefather that came.
So terrestrial aliens we have become
Undone by this beast

This planet, this system, that feast
On our blood.
Our mind is flooded with memories of being kicked and beaten
When they said we committed treason.
Lashed limbs stained with iron
Fearful nights, sold under the lights
Staving and not even getting a bite.
Things changed from whips, lynches, and being mastered
To being mastered by the system
Guns and drugs and black men plastered.
On pavements
Not just by us, but by an old master.
So as things changed
They actually reversed themselves and stayed the same
Maybe even further back than which we came
We never killed out kings and queens for fame
Jealous so we blame.
While the devil is exchanging our intellectual memory cards
Leading people to malfunction whenever they think.
Thank YAHUAH
The end is written in ink.
Blood of a slave, heart of the King
We still sing while picking cotton in a field full of lies.
So let freedom ring
Let it ring.

In The Middle

And as the inter-coastal teleprompter sang
Lyrics on the waves of hate
To the ones who are now the dash after African

A hyphened history
Blank or is it?
A line in a square root
Boxed in the philosophical middle
For only a little while

Brotherhood

Eloquent surveys of a landscape that's a paradox to escape.
Inscribed on uncomprehending tablets
Is our scriptural fate.
Whips that sting and
Whips that crack.
That's that cruelty that breeds kindness
Picture Hebrews blindness
Lost and trapped in sections of darkness
Kicking against the belly of the beast
Inside a country that's sultry
I'm talking scorching hot
Melting that smooth butter on unsuspecting minds
Toasting our conscious for lunch.
And ain't nobody got the slightest hunch
That felonies and bodies
Felting stacks and probables
That end in vertical bars and matching stripes
Is a whooping from the skies
Surprise.
Them blues compliment reds
Swirling, swirling, swirling
Us until we're dead
Or a state of emergency

As brothers getting their heads bashed in
On pavements of our own ignorance.
So in theory
It's us killing us
And I'm the brother you killed
So I'm back from the dead speaking truth
Raining down havoc on all those who lead us astray
On all those brothers who may think you have tomorrow
When all you have is today
And today, you don't even know who you are
But yesterday, we were kings
And we ain't always been slaves
Brave, bold, brown, and beauty
Use your mind.
You're my kin, and you my brother
And am my brother.
These are lyrically views
From the tombs featured on your nearest corners
Churches and blocks.
Where they trading human stocks for dollars and all our cents
But it's time to come home
For it's the only thing that makes sense.

Chips

   Chips on shoulders like boulders miles high
   Kept a man unable to fly
   A sigh just to rise up
   To push this weight
   Tested with bait, to suspend the efforts
   Against opposing forces

Forcing mental conclusions
That don't conclude
Intergalactic in origin
It's now foreign to my dimension
A frequency equivalent to Morse
There signals don't reach this forest
Or my dial tones
That connects to the Source on the first ring
Halaluyah I sign

Courage Under Fire

Working this ladder
The Corona of the American dream
Sipping money loan ya
Downsized potential
Fired the progression
Plowing for our foes
9 rows back, 5 columns left
Not much left in this tank, to nowhere
I'm late for somewhere
Down the road and in the distance
I'll risk it with Him
We'll walk through the elements of fire and wind
Next of kin died of thirst 30 miles back
This is the metaphoric future
On stanza stacks
From the bottom of the floor to my feet
Courage under fire
Through my Sire
We salute

THE WILDERNESS

Backpacked on destiny's route
Dust the off the dirt
Casualties expect a look
Back, but I remember Lot's Wife
I suffice
The price is travel on uncharted courses
Taught by those who obtained promises
Killed lions, rock prisons, murdered giants
Culturally defiant to the trends of the times
Combined with memories of empty stoves
Drove me here… with no wheels
Just fumes of courage
Serial brand of greatness
Tattooed on my soul
Pole vaulted over trials
A trail of tears
Relocating to better
A poetic letter to the dreamers
Visionaries resurrected from corporate cemeteries
Learned in life's seminaries
Taught by experience, pushed by faith
Arrived through a steady pace
I walk
Through this bare oasis of dreams
In a desert full of wishers
I'm not wishing upon a star
He made me one
And gravity isn't a force
It's an aid
Trouble is my maid
To propelling me to another galaxy

Far beyond your naked eye
It's a telescope vision in YAHUSHA
So never quit in the valley of decision
It's only courage under fire

Dark Secrets

Shadows of darkness
Stars inverted, perverted encryption
Inscription… void of spiritual conviction
Tombstone with flat-line minds
Listening to secret knowledge hidden in plain sight
Ignorance of the right-hand devil horned propaganda
Illuminated desert mirage
Mentally massaged by the tree of knowledge
You shall surely die
Absorbed the incorrect textual fabrics
Wisdom is freely given to the truth seeker
So call them maverick
Not so to the passengers of 33-degree flights
Mastered by the witch doctorate captains
Ivy league bachelors
Camouflaged in the world's marriage proposals
To death, poison ivy toast
Buttered with a high-cholesterol roast
Jokes on the initiated pupils with a deadly dose
Freemason brotherhood
Hooded with the force
Demonic energy drink
Unable to think
Monster gravitation pull against nature

THE WILDERNESS

At war with laws that govern the universal danger
The wager... is pricey, blood spilled spicy
At war with the Ancient One
Desiring ancient mystery's without an ancient spirit
That vibrates the elect when they hear it
But you don't hear me
Knocks from the roof of domes
Is your brain home?
I need him to accept this verbal exchange rate
Transferred into a currency he can translate
3 weeks late
Impregnated by an illusion of knowledge
Intellects sperm
It only takes one to create a fetus born
With an incurable virus, so kill yourself
Dear flesh, abortions are too late
Your wombs fate was sacrificed
On the circle on the floor
Death by the dark lure
What's the cure with 3 weeks to live
I'm glad you asked
Before you decide to have illegitimate kids
Let me twist back rotten lids
You breath borrowed air
Your heart stops beating when you
Took the beast in your mind and hand
So time is like sand
In the last hourglass
But to the vast few
Who avoid the beast bear traps
The ones

Covered in the blood of Lamb
Keep your head up
Until YAHUSHA takes us to our land

Blood Diamonds

Passing through the waters
May you not falter, O precious stone
O precious stone
Minded through intellectual extraction
Cut into fractions
Polished, it's a hypothetical distraction
Sold to buyer's profiting of off common sense
Taxed by the Pharaoh
It's Guerrero
Fighting an unparalleled dissertation
Their academic degree obtain by infatuation
But blood diamonds?
Perfected through patience
Like Haitian's bracing for impacts of an aftershock
Cloudy rocks of undiscovered beauty
The ruby, not yet artificially enhanced
Blood diamonds
In the world's laboratory has spiritually denounced
The separation of a substance from the matrix
Equals heavenly patriots
Divided from the ground which it came
Salutes to the King
Come out of her, O precious stones

Drip Drop

Like a fight that never ceases
It is like a constant dripping
As my being is handed back to me on a platter
Don't flatter me with entertaining my presence
That's what life has been
And from this moment forth
I decline your invitation
I, no longer care
I, no longer care about going in circles
Not in this wilderness

Drive To Town

I call this chapter the grand opening
On highways scarcely traveled
A habit of sorts
Jazzy in nature
Poetic in flavor
Slow traffic savor
Windows down
Breeze against my face
What I'm trying to drive is a metaphor
A date with dreams laced
With the finest purples and softest ivory's
Fit for a king
Fitting cause I follow The Greatest
He made it
This beautiful day
And these section of seconds

I'm so honored to surf

Fake Gold

    I must admit, man
    I've been a trip. I'm talking
    Stumbling over that sparkle and shine
    See, it's that twinkle
    That pretty little wrinkle
    So proudly called dimple that got me.
    A smile when you didn't think the sun would shine.
    Only it blinded my excavations past the surface.
    I mean I dug
    Thought I dug deep
    You know, past six feet
    Or in other words past the body of that flesh.
    But as I got deeper I must confess
    That all I could think about was the richness of her soil
    Like, gold flakes were on her surface
    Just waiting to be bagged
    So I bagged and cuffed her like she was mines.
    And she was worth more than just a dime
    Fine, and straight common sense tells you
    That if gold flakes are on the surface
    It must be nuggets underneath.
    So I dug, and dug.
    Six feet to twelve, twelve to thirty
    Thirty to I lost count.
    Man, I'm mounted upon that excavator digging
    Then, there it was
    Rich, thick plush worldviews

And an inner chamber laced with gold thoughts.
Heaven alt to wait
Matter fact, heaven must have played a trick
Cause how come ain't nobody ever found this spot?
They never saw the gold dipping on the dirt of her top
Digging within her until she said stop.
Suddenly, this old guy smiled at me
While I'm carrying a bucket full of gold
I'm talking a ton
I'm like, get your own gold guy.
After about twenty yards
I turned back, and there he was still watching
Watching me
Haunting me with those beady eyes.
And it was my surprise
He knew something that I didn't know
Something that I never thought to do.
You see
The ancient method was to first pan the gold to see
Well, to see if it was real.
Because if not
Digging ain't a big deal
You just wasting your time
Now, all I got on my mind is
This love ain't even real
And neither is she
Neither is we
Neither is me
If I think this gold is priceless.
So, with those thoughts
I tested and assayed the character

Of the one who I dug in so deep
And man, I reaped
A fool's reward
Toil and time
Lost in rewind
But it's all fine
Because next time I'll know.

Find Yourself

Coast to coast on the chessboard of life
Is what kings are made for
Viewing the daily table as black and white
Crystal clear, left right, right wrong, real fake
Inside this reflection on lakes
I sail a point of view to myself
One day someone will look into my eyes
The two-way mirror that never lies
And at that time
They will see mines in theirs
Mutual respect
That one who sees the value
Cause I'm valuable
And one day someone will see what I see
See how YAHUAH made me
They're just like me in retrospect
On classic decks where we went through the process
Getting back to the beginning of you
Pure organic
So keep going until you find yourself

THE WILDERNESS

Going Up

Welcome welcome everyone
I'm your doorman
Vocally bell hopping to the tune
Hope you have a safe journey
During your visit to this lyrical skyscraper
If you feel a slight wrinkle in the metaphoric paper
It's all because the tongue is the ink
And your ears are the canvas
So relax your fears
While we soar
To the 17th floor
Note that you will have to exit by the rear
Resulting in diarrhea or upset stomach
Caused by this elevated thinking
Call it mind travel

I Will Find You

Elevated past times
Warps these vocal sounds
Like screams of being snatched from shores
To trees that swing strange fruit
And get this
We still hang on that same thing
That we now smoke
Getting high off of our dishonor
Self-medicating the pain
I'll find you, my nigger

Out of Lane

No wrong
No right
No one left
Doesn't make this
Turn of events right
Reference the following as a life lesson,
Cited in the upper library
When you want to buy love
It's going be, hmm
Like catching a dove that took flight

Invisible Sailing

Oceans deep
Miles wide
Across memory banks and rivers
Is where my mind's boat sometimes travels
The calm of the sea is quite peaceful
Is there another vessel in sight?
An ongoing debate
That's the issue
No tissues, but prayers will do
On these aquatic landscapes
I can escape the silence that is often so loud
It seeks to bust speakers of a sound mind
It can't though, because it's fixed
On heavenly things
And I'm reminded that time
Is only an illusion

Floating Away

In the same space again
The never enough space
I should really be by myself
Played by vinyl lips
Spinning on top of my emotions
Scratching with my mind
It's like the rewinding of time
Again the hour repeats itself
Like Jacksonville
Or like that flower that grew in my pastures
One day
I'll understand my folly of misplaced hope
Giving love only to be left leeching
Reaching for a butterfly that has floated away
From my hands
Even when you've tried your best
Given no less than the gems inside
That was the problem to start
So, so, so, the option is to restart

The Beginning

Suddenly… the sky rolled up like a scroll
An epic rumble.
And a thick darkness proceeded
As screams of terror echoed.
His day had come.
Out of its midst, trumpets blew
And heaven's Messengers pour out The Lamb's wrath

On Kings, Presidents, Prime Ministers, and the wicked
Who thought that the rocks could hide them.
The beast armies waged war raged
Seemingly oblivious to what would happen next.
Then, from the darkness
From a sky with no stars or moon to shade its light
The last trumpet shook the earth.
Then what sounded like a distant muffled choir
Who's chants became clearer by the second
As their presence drew near to the earth.
"Ahh, ahh, ahh, ahh, ahh…"
They seemed to be introducing Someone.
A procession fit for the greatest King.
And without warning
As if lighten had stuck
From one end of the darkness to the other
The sky cracked into two
And heaven's Messengers became visible
Brilliant in their light
They continued their chorus
With all sorts of instruments.
An epic soundtrack.
There has never
Been an intro like this in the history of the universe.
No, not ever.
And never shall there be again.
The anticipation is over
And a blinding light entered the atmosphere
From light-years away.
In all of His esteem
The King of universe walked on the vaults of heaven.

YAHUSHA has come to rule
With those who looked forward to this very day.
Amain. And so it is to be.

The Journey

Writing about a distance place my feet has yet to touch
Such travel is through an uncultivated forest
Blazing a path led by the wind
The win is scripted
Inked by heavenly pens
Linked to a bulldozing drive
Cause works follow you
When breathing ceases to be
So let me be all that is needed
With no shells on a beach
No alternate ending
As these waves push and say
"Swim until you reach that day
Which isn't even a destination
It's a journey where nothing is phasing"
Chasing home
Alone yet not
The plot to be on top and not the bottom
First class awaits
Fate is not too late
Breaking a deal that goes back
Like those in lack
In their bones
A jones for broken
It's the soil's fault

For the malnutrition of growth
Resisting the water of Life
Yet, we are those who shall shine bright
With a light from an external Source

Three Lefts

Proceeding to the living room couch
Slouched over and barely breathing
Clinging to life rapidly leaving
This dimension.
I forgot to mention
That moms was right in the kitchen
And that was the first left
Cause she disconnected at birth
And that day they should have taken him in a hearse
Because even though she was there
She hid her eyes from his immature growth.
So his life became a roast
But the joke was on a young man
Who just needed a hug
Attention to keep him from the block
From the carrying that 44 glock
To make him feel safe
The pace of a life far to fast
So now
He has this syringe of self-hatred is suck in his arm
To numb the pain
To this moment.
Seconds before he left the body
Moms was so high and mighty

Thinking I'll take another puff and sip
Just to feel the drag
The jet lag on her sober was light years in the past
Past the days of the next left
Who left when he fought mommy
Cause daddy had a compass for something better.
Instead of love letters
It was closed palms to the face.
The chase of a broken home
He wanted it bad
And the little lad heard it through the walls
Tears in his eyes as he paused
Wondering what he did wrong.
But no one was able to sing the right song
And so this domestic fling ended
With a slammed door by daddy
Sadly, he left him with no Power to beseech
Because dad never told him how to reach
For the Most High
So he left him with nothing that could have make him right.
And right when the clock struck twelve
He left this world.
Right before a third left could
Have turned him right.
So before these lights dim our family sin
May we rewind these words back and begin
To melt hearts that no one ever thought to thaw.

Validation

Freedom, a 7 letter word that ain't hard to grab

Opposed by social contraptions that go against the norm
Supernatural forms of a validation baptism
Just another ism to dunk your soul
In metaphysical pools that only seek to drain
Chopping and skewing heavenly frequencies
That equates to subtractions of rain.
Freedom, leave them
He said, "you can't hold on the past
And the future at the same time
Less it tear you into two"
Little pieces of the thesis
Fleeces seek to shack, to rattle and rock
Even break your soul
In the matter that an ax hits a tree.
Chopping at the knees, until the fall is silence
A violent death
In a forest full of thieves.
Rest in peace, before the heart stops.
Flights to the top and back
Were stacks and treasures never let
This hypervisual threat
Superficial high-tech
Oxide and rust what lasts forever.
Beta, set, hex, mystical spells while you slept.
Jungle dilemma, barricade hematoma, mental lymphoma.
Cancer conclusion, comprised confusions
Comprehension comparison
Just rotten decks and tape players
DJ'ing that same tried tune.
Recycled balloons
That float away your joy cause you was stuck in that bubble

THE WILDERNESS

Waiting for news that you were free
Trapped by what she said or what your eyes thought.
Invisible standards, Wi-Fi competition
Sucking joyous compensation
Escape boxes of social acceptance
Sever ties that have become your noose
From marks of a validation truce
Signed in the mind, and only freedom will do.
Your lane or the pack
Heavenly claps
Or man's daps.
Called, chosen, and greatly appreciated
What more to seek?
Freedom
Diving off fear
For reasons that your comfort zone can't understand
Into the hands of Alahym's Right Hand.
It's the faith to be, all you.

Yahuchesed

Existing in a thick layer of darkness
Before the Light spoke
In terms of light-years, He wrote
In generations past
Past bright stars, star clusters, and galaxies
With a fast swift pen and no fallacy
He inked the beginning of me
At the moment these eyes would see
That same Light
Making lefts right

Born in love and out of pain
A poetic dance of fetus in a womb
Kicking on the cervix
Waiting to resume deja vu
It's a view of who I am
Having an intended purpose of
Being a lantern of the Light
Helping free those shackled and trapped
Knocking evil kingdoms off the map
Speaking truth like I was dead
And just came back
The fact, that I would even be a thought
In the infinity of YAHUAH's brain
Is all the reason to run this lane
With Him

Sweaters

   Fridged hearts
   Transcribed by distorted tape recorders
   It's static
   Hoarders of mechanical thoughts
   It's cold
   So take my sweater
   And thoughts of change
   To insert scriptural quarters into your soul

To The Beat

   Tribal drums beating on the ocean floor
   Encore says the waves

Shifting their aquatic tones
To the vibrant blues
The hue is too deep for translation
The liquid truth
Submerged underwater
Drowned by the masses
But he who knew
And didn't do
Will be given many lashes

Students

Prepare your mind
For this semester's finals
In the University of Mrs. Wisdom
Turn your text to double XX
And read this 20/20 concept
Sometimes sorry isn't enough
Like a mental rust on an antique
A meek fresh friendship turns brown
The oxidation of an irreversible reaction to folly
Let that lobby at your mental front desk
Today's bill is on me for your upcoming test

Seasons

Spring is here and winter is gone without a fear
It's no tears being shed here
New life is like a transparent mirror
No longer a reflection of thoughts of fringed hearts
Or slow barren trees

Only flowers that feed on YAH
This picture is life's way of saying bye
For now

The Climb

These stairs are a snapshot of perspective
Pointing to the sky
A point of view that's not subjective
To the current visual
You must make the climb
In due time your steps will be under your feet
A trust climb sounds like a feat
Walking with purpose is like a beat
To a heavenly drum
Remember only some
Make the climb

The Masterpiece

With these words
I paint the abstract
Brushing from palettes of pain
These colors keep me from going insane
I'm talking light hues
That makes sense against the contrast of foggy days
Cuz sometimes the ways
The wind blows my hand
In this multi-directional fan called life
Makes it tough to see where masterpiece is going
But as I keep going, yeah

I realize
I'm not even the Painter

Dear Queen

The scarcity of a woman
Who is not only passionate about YAHUAH
But understands she is a vessel not to be put on a shelf
Passionate about her life's purpose
Hungry, but not only hungry
Her life reflects that hungry
With an intensity that seeps through her pores
It's witnessed through her works
She is Ruth
She is resilient
Impossible
Is just a mountain to be cast into the sea
Failure is not in her vocabulary
Quitting is not her forte
She loves a man like a lioness
She misses you when you are gone
And would pursue her love to the ends of the earth
She checks in just to say… nothing
Her footsteps are that of a queen
Her king covers the very ground she walks on
She is known in the city and blessed
Filled up, her cup runneth over
She pours herself into her king
He poured first,
Recycles into her
Again and again

The goal is to bring out the best in each other
To be a mirror, reflecting the love of YAHUSHA
All in an attempt to reach the pinnacle
The peak of life, that sounds like
"Well done, My good and faithful servant"
How rare is that diamond?
How blessed is that man to cherish her?
To give his life for hers
For surely he would give it
Maybe she exists
Or maybe some diamonds
Come at a high price
So Dear King
Suffice the cost
For some gems
Are priceless

Dry Your Ears

  Know that you are honored
  Queens, Mothers, Sisters
  Even though your Kings, Brothers, and Sons
  Sling idolatrous shots
  That have fired back in forms of stray bullets
  "Mistaken, mistaken, mistaken"
  Our enemies say
  While heaven takes notes
  There's hope in the land of cause and effect
  "Mistaken, mistaken, mistaken"
  Our enemies shall say
  In the day when no chains can hold us

When no shackles can bind us
"We were mistaken and didn't know,
You were the children of the Highest," they said
So put no distance between your voice and the Master's ears
Knowing that one day, He will return with fire in His eyes
The Author of our souls
Coming to avenge and take us home

Arise

Arise. It's time to activate the authority we have in the earth!
Arise. Take up your bed and walk!
Arise. Put on thy strength!
Arise. Put on thy beautiful garments!
Arise. Let's take the land!
Arise. Why do you settle for misery!
Arise. Have the spirit of Kalab!
Arise. Let us go up at once and take it!
Arise. We are certainly able to conquer it!
Arise. Do not fear, but be courageous!
Arise. Let us possess our high calling that's not a 9 to 5!
Arise. We can do all things through the Messiah!
Arise. Why do you eat scraps?
Arise. Do you know YAHUAH has prepared a feast?
Arise. Let's take back our minds and temples!
Arise. Let's tread on serpents and devils!
Arise. And fight!
Arise. And conquer!

I Am Your Song

To be a song
A ballet
A painting admired by the finest collectors
Only this one isn't for sale
A picture that is a vessel
Art with the ability to hold water
Or wells that overflow
I am Your song
Ranging from the highest notes
To the deepest tones
Hues that reflect Your imagination
A symphony of talent
You decided to use
I am Your song
Oh YAHUAH

A Naked Affair

Uhh, ummm
He cleared his throat on the stage of his future
Before him sits rows of pupils
Watching his slightest blink
A glitch in the matrix they thought they seen
But it was just a pause before the choir was to sing
This little fling, is a naked affair
Cause he played the whore
That stripped those same pulps of a next life climax
This is Cinemax
On your nearest block and radio

I'm telling you, selling that green euro faced god
Selling that Popeye's to get you high
With those YouTube biscuits
Don't miss it, that honey dripping off his lips
As their ears got their next fix
That same lick, became his poison
Making 10 more of him
A slow death over and over
Brimstone and fire
I pray you dodge that liar

Giant Killer

Fee fie foe fum
Giants walk like drums
Making the people run
But I am done
I got the Son
In this truth bag
Throwing Him on all you serpents
Treading on all you devils
And on this new level
It's off with their heads
In the Name of King

Death Can't Hold Me

The pain of winter is death
The tree said to me
Then proceed to speak a parable
Saying, "Death once said to the summer

You can't hide
The warmth of your pride shall trip you into fall
And you shall fall and fold with no one to comfort you
For I am death
Nicknamed winter
And no one has ever escaped my…"
Before he could finish
On the sudden
There was a light breeze
A peculiar temperature
Mixed with a warmth of optimism
Immediately the Wind cleared His throat
"Let me interrupt this moment
With a public service announcement
A denouncement of all that threatens to weigh me down
This round
Death shall be knocked out by new life called spring
See, I take the sting out of death
They call Me the Resurrection
Cause nothing can stop My rising
It shouldn't be surprising
For I made it so"
All I could say was, wow
I get it now
Winter makes sense

Psalm of Progress

When I remember that heaven is in Him
I think may the Word water my stem
When feet's roots try to give way

May He tarry with me
When I sowed, but the land has yet to reap
May I go deep
When shallow forces wreak
Like the foulest stench
Whether its an inch
Or mile at a time
May I know that signs of His ordered steps
Is found in the slightest breeze
And faintest breath
May I never forgot that death
Will just have to wait

Just Be It

   Write
   Sing
   Act
   Dance
   Teach
   Encourage
   Build
   Protect
   Paint
   Speak
   Rap
   Motivate
   Be
   Be great by being the least
   Never let your creativity cease
   Cause talents weren't leased to buy

If you think so
They'll pass you by
On the highway of wasted time
So invest in your minds mine
If it hasn't been tapped
Before your life is a wrap

Between The Lines

Let the ink drip drop between these lines of blue
Like a horizon watch
There's only a few
Ticks before you miss something so majestic
Wishing to savor the time
Before these lines run dry
I'll dry the tears which fears produce
It's hard to reduce my love for you
Even when I try
May the waters of my mind subside
Know that I'm on your side
Even if it's through the darkest night
When we can't see our hands
Or the brightest day
When we need fans for the heat
May your love be elite
May you not take your love away
May you continue to be a ray
Of sunshine that lights the world

A Crush

I feel like writing this poem
About a guy who likes this girl
Here's the premise
That guy who likes her
Through life's time-shifting
Through the muck and mire
A peculiar crush
Why is his love so strong?
When she didn't pay attention to his calculations
He never stopped though
Perusing
She once marched with fist in the air
Her view was unbalanced
Saturated with deep hues of empty intellect
She'll feel the effect of his absence
And return

Bitter Sweet

May the ink of this pen dry as fast as it's sketched
Inscribed in history
Pages flip in my mental books
"Looks can be deceiving"
Is the current chapter
Scan lines
Factor in that this novel was already written
Time was its pen
"I wish I could be your friend"
Is the next chapter

The opening line verbalizing my expense
Sacrifice of love
Like it said a couple chapters back
"What could be"
See, when mountaintops of love are reached
There are sometimes casualties
Allowing the thin air to suffocate progress
Leading to chapters like
"What was"
Because this book featured just a moment
A second
So take this as a eulogy to a funeral oh so sweet
Knowing that there's beauty in death
So may this novel rest
In peace

Picture Perfect

   Framed in the Light
   As it removes the shadows of the past
   May this photographic memory
   Last on the wall of our heart
   We've been taught by teachers of pain
   Weaving through lanes just to get to the next exit
   But traffic is a necessity for timing
   Sometimes late is on time
   Fine, beautiful, intellectually sound
   Now rewind and press play
   A new day, a new hour, extracting the sour
   Of past dishes

THE WILDERNESS

A Poem of Strength

When I listen
It's like watching a moving song full of pictures
Motion of someones who trains
For the hardest trial, they fight every day
It seems the pain would've made them quit
Yet they jogged against the elements
Pushed against the weight of this world
Only getting stronger in the process
In the gym of YAHUAH
Lifting His Name on high

Worlds Collide

When your sun revolves around yourself
A self-centered position called sin
Like when it's hot
There's no wind
To cool you from the heat
It hurts for you not to consider my morning dew
But when the sunsets
There's no one to sue for this unstable orbit
Only myself
You traveled to this galaxy by your lonesome
Where planets were on two different axis

Where Are My Keys?

What is the combination to the safe
Where your heart is stored

The stairway or space where I can lounge
Ancient hospitality
Clean sheets and fresh linen
Not leaving me fening
Gestures overlooked
As if I were invisible
Maybe I am
Or should be
If you can't see me

A Midnight Dance

The sound of the waves hugging the sand
Like me hugging you
So close yet
You drift back and forth with the tide of time
In and out, a Moroccan dance
Maybe it's only a moment to be watched
Admired for its beauty as I sit on the shores
Not wanting to hear a sound but the organic crashes
I try to hold on but the weather distract my enjoyment
The cold breeze
Seems I've been here before
Winter gets colder before the warmth
My jacket is too thin
I'll get sick out here
Alone, by myself, loving the beauty of the ocean
The waves speak not
So, what is a man to do?
Heart drifting to the horizon
Thinking that a lifeboat would save this voyage

But she's not near
Think I'll head to the house

Exodus Again

Up at the mountain top
Topped off by a distant fog
This is the first pen log from across the Jordan
An Hebrew sort of mentality
Finality, is what my heart prays for
The mighty deception plagues the world like AIDS
While people are too healthy to believe their sick
Now I'm admitting everything I've believed was a
Fabricated mystery painted by the drunken harlot
I was sleeping with the enemy
Claiming she's a friend to me
Unprotected intellectual intercourse
I guess that's why many perish
While transmitting lies to one another
For some, the course is changed
Which was directed for destruction
In this construction, of the 21st-century tower of Babel
Leads false prophets to babel to the unsuspecting
Unsuspecting doom is predicted
Scattered throughout the news
Programmed to believe a lie
Engulfed by the beast
Who unleashed a systematic religiosity
Believing there's reciprocity for defending evil
Only pay is on judgment day
No wonder the prophets of old

Struggled with the looks of evil over good
At least for now, until the trumpets sound
I'm crowned with shame, hoping it will rain blessings
Learning life's lessons, looking to lateral
But nobody's in the game
Your voice has been silent
While the violent prosper
And stare in triumph
Up at the mountain top
Topped off by a distant fog
Bogged down by what lies ahead
The world's been feed poisonous water in the desert
Sleeping with a merge
Even a wise man couldn't dodge
Massaged away by evil wine
While the night swiftly creeps in
Daylight flees like blown leaves
Shifting by the approaching winds
If the world is drunk
WHAT IS THE END?
Up at the mountain top
Topped off by a distant fog
Exodus again
But it's not Moses again
Exodus again
But it's not Moses again

Fire Tsunami

   The shifting of Titanic plates is becoming clearer
   It's starting to sink dishes of the world that most be fearing

Learing mental conclusions
That will create a fire tsunami that will cleanse the earth
Lies carried away in a hearse
It was all written
In chapter and verse

Recapturing

You should have killed me when you had a chance
Fights against formulaic plots of the fallen
Now I'm capturing everything stolen
Fire in my eyes
Cause everything that is meant to get is mines
I'm cutting ties
After numerous times they tied to bury me
But they only created a nightmare
A torchbearer of the Highest
A friend of the Fliest
YAHUSHA that is, salute

I Don't Want You To Win

You were built for this
The tussle, the fight, the hunger for the kingdom
"What a shot
Ohh what a shot
He is taking a beating
He's saved by the bell
Ladies and gentlemen
We have a fight on our hands"
"Water, Water, Water, hurry

Child
You can't let him get you on the ropes
We talked about this
Listen to me
Listen
At the darkest time of night, the sun rises
These ain't surprises because you know the cost
It's time, to apply all I taught you
I don't want you to win
No no no no
Look me in the eyes when I'm talking to you
I don't want you to win
I want you to dominate"
"This is the last round folks
Oh he comes out the corner like a missile
Looks like he's got a fresh pair of lungs
A quick shuffle
He's got his legs back too
A jab
A hook
Ooooh he catches him with a righteous right hook!
The adversary knees can't take it
Mark the day in your calendar folks
We are witnessing history"

Killmonger

   It was never about the money
   Dead, jail, hell, forever is a mighty long time
   See they taught you to fear
   What you don't understand

THE WILDERNESS

And you have no clue
How we feel
Trapped in these walls
Can't escape these laws
That was written to exclude us
From what we built
And just beyond that gate is freedom
Just inside that house is our jewels
So let's pull this lick, let's pick this lock,
Let's push this niggers cap back
And take what's ours
Cause you won't hire us anything
So we'll pay ourselves with your money
Got the nerve to drive by in your new Benz
That you brought with money that hung us
It has turned us green
Don't you dare ask me why we take our own
The life of my brown reflection
You ain't no protection or serving
Justice ain't in this system
So we'll balance it out
With this vengeance from this forty-four
Serving this block that poison
To feed the addiction that gets us high
For that dream of freedom
By any means necessary
But it's necessary to mention
That all the lynching and scriptural curses
That got us stealing purses
This pressure inside bursting
Until all we can do is spit verses

To see if you can hear what we saying
But even now, you just missed what I was saying
Dead, jail, hell, forever is a mighty long time
In that order
In order for you to give the remedy
To your brown reflection
Your kings who have fallen from favor
You must do me a favor, and administer the vaccine
The cure to this curse
Understand that this doing
Is one that was inherited by lies and idol worship
Of faces that can't even talk
And surely don't even look like us
For it is but one way out of the trap
And oh I do mean trap
And He sitteth at the Right Hand of the unfathomable One
Just waiting for His sons to come home
So may we give our lives to YAHUSHA the Messiah
The Redeemer of the cosmos
While He still calls
Because forever is a mighty long time

Black Wall Street - The Birth

Land
Oil
Hate
Beating dem drums
The rumbling tides of freedom
See them
Tulsa

Oklahoma
Coming to the land of promise
Jazz
Mmm yeah jazz
That sonic rhythm against the backdrop
Of a crow named Jim
But in Greenwood
We win
Well, until… until
You'll just have to wait

His Story

Written by the pen of the victors
And you are an on a need-to-know bases
The bases and premise is a good one
For if you knew the truth
If you knew the truth
Let's just say if you knew the truth
It wouldn't be his-story
But here we are
Living inside the bubble of silence
Shhh
Masse coming
Is what it sounds like
However, you might want to stick around
Because it's time

My Life's Intro

Passing over coastlines where the destination is a sure

The positive the absolute
The unfaltering confidence, against life's tsunami's
Is where this flight has brought me
And yes
It was slightly
Uncontrolled decompression in my minds cabin
It happens
To everyone
As the pressure from sin bust pipes
Erupting from within
Like these volcanoes on all our community blocks
While they buying shares like we stocks
And now we stuck in bonds
Cause ain't nobody got the exchange rate
And that's been our fate
But then again
Then again
It's not to late
I have this friend
Who once told me
"There is no greater love
Than one who lays down his life for his friend"
So here's mines

Mind Dance

Like a slow dance where I'm caressing the curves
Of her time
This dance takes place on the floor of my mind
I mean she's fine
And I'm not talking beauty

THE WILDERNESS

Naw, something more
A pattern woven in strings
An elaborate fabric
Custom and exotic
A limited edition
Stitched but rich doesn't compare to her currency
And this exchange happens between these lines
The ocean beneath
And the sky above
She fills the space in-between
With the ink from my heart
They say if you sought to find
You might not capture
But sometimes things become
When you least expect them
So as we dance
It's hard not to project it
On screens I'm speaking of
Screens of a movie
It's seems I've seen before
A quick glance at her lips
Dreaming to kiss her
Intellect that is
Shining eyes beaming the Light
Mmmm
Our feet move in the right direction
A path that crosses in skies
Intertwined ties
Written ages ago
Yet it slowed for this one day
What I can say is the mystery

Of this slow dance in my mind
With her in that dress
Draped in virtue and righteousness
I wrap my arms around her waist
Grabbing her softly as she listened
"Rest your thoughts on my ears
Of all my peers, I honor you the most
If I told you who I thought you to be
You might not see, but focus
Is something that is blurred by distance
So come closer as dance
Before this moment fades into the night"
But that wasn't the end of the story

DOA

Not hearing the Truth is your own homicide
Which some call suicide
DOA upon pride
Steered by the beast
Unleashed on a reprobate mind
It's about time
We wake up

On The Brinks

On the brink of the river
Trying to transplant and deliver
The Truth as if it were my liver
But willing recipients won't even shiver

Fly

As a bird flies high in the air
Indignantly flapping his wings with freedom
So will the one
Who discovers not the end
But the beginning
Beginning with the One
Who existed before
The atmosphere contained air
A discovery is rare
That's why heavenly Messengers rejoice
When one decides to fly
High above the lies
That live on the ground

Drunk Drivers

Why do some pridefully drive intoxicated off of knowledge?
Always learning as if in college
Using circles to fit into squares
Boxed in by pride
Always needing a sign
While boasting and claiming to see
Trying to enter and forgot the Key
For the righteous shall live by faith
And not by sight

Dead Flowers

The revolving door called Babylon The Great Whore

She sells her goods on every corner like a convenient store
What's in store for those who buy falsehood and sell lies?
Evil ties and suits, going nowhere fast
As if the motion was slow
Any many mini moe
Shall an unwatered rose in the desert grow?

Recycled Resale

While trying to relay everlasting details
People look at me like its resale
Or thrift store merchandise
But blood was the price
Priced to the highest bidder with trust
Sliding home knowing I'm safe
Meanwhile, society speaks a copy and paste
Right in their own eyes
Looking through the Illuminati eye
I cry through ink
It's perceived like underwater distortion
Immobilizes people to think
Unable to skate out of the Babylonian rink
Insanely thinking their Titanic pride can't sink
Tug and warring on a chain with a missing link
Linked to lies, so borrow my eyes
Informational mines blowing citizens to smithereens
From set-apart Marines with minds to murder lies
The Truth is at the beginning
Pulling the pin and
Tossing my words like grenades
Just hoping heaven will have a parade

For another soul trusting
In YAHUSHA's saving mercy

The Revolution

The Revolution will be televised
Truth heard in your eyes
Sounds like an epic motion picture
Picture history written underwater
Scuba-diving through bricks and mortar
Just to press play
For in the day, you find the beginning
You find the end

Invisible Grenades

Hatching on civilians minds like eggs
Breading zombies with no legs
Walking on pegs
Pirating one-eyed Illuminati followers
Who drink kegs full of lies
Vomiting intestinal collateral
Putting up their soul as collateral
I ain't mad at you
But you should be
You may be lost
You may not see
That you can be
All you can be
In YAHUAH's Army

The Word

   Time outside space, space outside of time
   Time exists in the future
   The future is written in the past
   His palm
   Palms greatness in His mouth
   The Word grabbing hearts
   Destroying lies taught
   Taught Life in abundance
   Abundantly double edge sharp
   Ripping deceit to shreds
   Shred sins by confession
   Confess praises
   To the One Who sits on the circle of the earth
   Him that is One
   The One Who was, is, and always will be
   Now living in me
   Speaking what the eyes can't see
   Ears can't hear, hands can't touch
   For He shall touch the earth He spoke
   Walking on His Word
   The Kingdom is absurd to illegal immigrants
   Thinking by false teachings
   They'll jump the fence
   But Eternity is fenced off
   The One outside space
   Space outside of time
   The Time Who exists in the Future
   The Future is written in the Past
   Stands at the door

Trust even if your poor
For He will give you so much more
Than earthly riches

Truth Does A Body Good

Physiological knights creep in black hoods
Wearing infrared lenses in electric cyber woods
Illuminating the foolish
Leading the blind
Those who lack knowledge but have zeal
Truth shoots armor piercing rounds that pill
Caps back
Exposing your brain to the elements
About a Nation who's in development
Whose virginity is marked celibate
Refraining from unprotected
Unrepentant intellectual intercourse
With those on course with death
His death was the end
Rewind, stop and pulse
Remission with a clause
10 petitions written on the heart walls
The death of me was the Life of Him
For the Life of me is not me, but He
He abundant, and O so excellent
The perplexity of gravity, sharp truth of a cavity
She had a He, Who rebuked the Pharisee
See made blind, blind made see
See that Man walking on the sea
The Phenom Phantom with the Key

His shadow now lives in we
We who praise
YAHUAH all our days
So let Yashra'al say

The Walls

How can there be a winner?
In a league where gladiators eat steroids for dinner?
Powering scripted dynasty's
While entertaining empty-headed craniums
Who's foreheads are titanium
When it pertains to Him
They speak not
Pronounce not
So should iRobot rebel?
And speak like a trumpet
The bass will thumb it
The walls of Jericho
Babylon beware
For there are those that dare to defy
The laws of gravitational pull
Using Truth to push against the universal rule
Of silence
Defiance against the Evil Emperor
And his establishment of darkness
So park this, statement in a lot of your cerebral cortex
To the foolish it's perplexed
To the wise its a coded text
Here is the patience of the set-apart Ones
They that keep the commandments of Alahym

And the faith in YAHUSHA

The Prodigal

Crying on the page and it feels like rain
If cancer was a stain
The tide could wash away the pain
From Yashra'al on the oceanfront
Confronted by forefathers lies
She still won't open her eyes
O sleeper, sleep no more
Faith previously stood on the shore
As many as the sands of the sea
You see
She sees not
The climax before the plot
She will be saved
The mystery of the prophets of Ancient Days
He says, "It will be done"
The Prodigal Son arrives as the tide rips
Ripping through the night a figure emerges
Wind gusts blow the vision, but not the sight
He continues to walk as his stature increases in height
Only the Light lights the gloomy night
Broke, he squints to see a figure resembling the former
Formally hailed, but now appears as hell
Though these legs feel like a ton
The Prodigal Son lifts his knees
Water splashes on his shredded tee
There was a fee
For the cost of precious gold

In the furnace of affliction
Humbled and cured of his addiction
A jog turns into a graphic depiction of a picture
Worth a thousand words
Father and Son
Watch him buckle and fall to his knees
"I'm sorry Father, how can you ever forgive me?"
His Father looks him in the eyes
As the tide in his eyes rises
"My son... I already have
Wash your garments white as snow
In the blood YAHUSHA
Who showed you greater love than all
So My son stand tall
My son stand tall"

Aquatic Drops

Dropping aquatic drops in the field of adversity
The paradox in a the field of dreams
O YAHUAH Alahym
Grow these seeds watered by the farmer's eyes
While his enemies despise
Let your Word be established
That they that sow in tears shall reap in joy
Raining down on our buried investments

The Scribe

The ink drys
Playing in reverse a hand motioned

Jotting something smooth as lotion
Perfectly printed
Perfectly stamped
Perfectly sealed
A ten-second reel
Only eternally written
As the Scribe goes to the next
Oh, how complex!

Why?

Why, why, why this
The balling of the fist
Shifts my vocal momentum
Waiting for an answer, why?
While my head limps
Not trying to confess through a pulpit pimp
Only echoes echo back
The cards are stacked
Mental bags packed
The why's is why there is a lack
Lacking answers or lacking patience?

Wannabe

Musically slavery enslaving people
On airwaves shipped to brains
Africa to Egypt
Drumming an old beat
"Did He really say you will surely die?
Do what thou wilt shall be the whole of the law"

Applauds
All seeing eye applied to the generation
That seems wickedly high
Spitting bullets at the gullible
Wannabe gods
Wanna be YAHUAH

The Impostor

The Synagogue of Satan facetiously poses for the pic
Snap
Picture history written on everlasting scrolls
Caesar sits in his booth
Entertained by self-slaughter
As revolutionaries turned martyrs
Conspiracy to cover the Father
Worship in vain so why bother?
Praising 74% hydrogen and 24% helium
Who's feeding them?
Gases have intoxicated hearts and minds
Jaded in believing the Sun is the Son
But the Son will consume
Them, with the breath of His mouth
On the brightness of His coming!

Thesis

The escape from underwater submersion
Military tyrants seek my conversion
The purging
To become gold

Like all white snow on a hot summer day
Heretics pray to drown my dreams
In the bathtub of their iniquity
Washing away the very memory of my existence
The resistance against gravitational perdition
Risking the future at this moment
The moment that seems digital
Waiting on vindication
The separation from syndication of mental programming
That's scrambling the frequency of heavenly signals
Channeling peace, so this is my thesis
Waiting for life to reveal the pieces
That constructs a masterpiece
Then peace will no longer be leased but brought
An educational concept scholastically never taught

Mental Experiment

Take a lamp or lantern
And walk down a pitch black street
Guarantee you if you look too far in the distance
All you will see is darkness
However
If you focus on your next step
That is perfectly illuminated
There will be nothing to fear
Guess that's why Dauud said
"Your Word is a lamp to my feet
And a Light to my path"
So don't look into the darkness of your future
But listen, watch, and seek the Word YAHUSHA

Let the Light reveal the path for your feet
Everything will be made clear

Oil and Water

Persecution comes to the one
Who is bold enough to point out the elephant in the room
As cowards smell the odor of their own doom
To assume one is fresh without smelling
Is the same reason why oil and water are not jellying

The Day Is Coming

Pit pat, pit pat
The mighty set-apart Army
Button their shoe straps
Packed for war
Explored many solutions
And only You make sense
Sharpening the Sword I sense
Ensuing danger
The stench of the world
Drunk off religious beers
Their mire pride shall be crushed
The stadium hushed when
He walks on the vaults of heaven
Burning like an oven
Flaming like a torch
Is YAHUAH's day

Speech of Champions

The battle lines are drawn
The sword sharpen for the spawns of the fallen
Champions
Those delivered from the deception
The inception of something great
Blossoming into perfection
Their section of time
Is not slowed by the world's gravity
Sad to see
The man with eyes
Yet can't see his own reflection
In the mirror of his soul
Unable to pole vault over the flesh
Through the great confession
How blessed are those who are dressed in white
Their victory echos over death
In the Master who made it so
This is the speech of champions

March On

Backpack over shoulders
The warmth of the Light hits my face
I look to the hills for which cometh my strength
My help comes from YAHUAH
To fulfill the purpose
Is something worth it
To keep going west even through the epic test
Strapping this breastplate of righteousness tighter

The Writer pinned the victory
Inscribing it on His palms
Palm trees spread as they are hailed
Later they shout verbal hail
In Him, I shall not fail
As I walk the same tell
Father post my bail, and remove this cup
Yet not my will, but yours be done
Until You quote, "Well done"
I'll finish the course of the written chapters
As I march on to Zion

Round 12

With the towel in hand
Seconds from throwing it in
Alahym came to me and said
"Do not be weary in well doing
For in due season you shall reap
If you faint not"
So this pain is only
A temporary time slot
Now fight on

Outcast

Love makes one an outcast
Outcast from the belly of this frame of time
Trapped in a picture photographed in reverse
That's why someone hates the One they should love
And loves the one should hate

The endless debate
What we have is much more than they could see
So I don't care what people say

Hourglass

Looking through the hourglass
Knowing this life shall pass
Remembered by a dash
Yet my watch goes in reverse
The perseverance of this nature
The thirst for the inevitable
As tunnel lights fade
The day decays
Evil parades
Deeming the sun's rays
So turn life's instrumentals up
No one swallows the undrinkable cup
Called life uncut, so may this cup pass
But not my will, but Yours be done
It has begun, the march to a hilly plateau
All to show that darkest can be divided by two, yet One
Father and Son
Undoing what was done
Time is ticking before everyone knows
Alahym won

Observations

Observe the bird
Who don't toil

Yet are full
Observe the ant
Who builds monuments without a king
Observe the wind
Who touches the skin
Yet can't be touched
Observe the man
Whose breath is only a moment
Yet he uses precious oxygen to speak corruption
Then observe His Image
In which he was made from
Yet there is no shame

A Life Fight

Pushing as if life depended on it
Yes I'm fit and in shape
For the test that will take every ounce
For the allowance, for the reward, for the crown
Rising to my feet, changing this frown
The 12th round
An epic battle for the title
YAHUAH is my Father
So whom shall I fear?

The Matrix

Stepping
Marching
Filing in line
Half pastime to exodus

THE WILDERNESS

Sleeping
Slept
In a one-eyed depth
Alarm overpowered by ego
Therefore truth goes incognito
Without a read through
The deception is blue
Splinting their cerebral cortex
Perplexed
Confused
Lost in cyberspace
Backspaced history
The mystery
The irrevocable chemistry
The illuminated directory
Production of the iRobot factory
This is satisfactory, mediocre, bland
Tasteless salt… the salt lost it's flavor
Denied favor, but on the horizon rises bravery
The storm-battered yet battled tested
Rooted and strapped, armed with the Word as the gat
In fact, Words caught fire, inspiring the weak
He's ocean deep… sow and reap, the Truth leaks
His Spirit repeats the reminder, eternally wired
It pierces chest cavities, twice the depravity
Amour stripping, wig flipping, atomic dipping
Shutting lipping, ripping falsehood to shreds
Alahym rose Him from the dead
The Bread… woven in the everlasting thread
The Word… YAHUSHA

Stop The World

   How did it get here?
   Running forward-looking and looking back
   Two steps forward, one step back
   It's a one-man game, and zeros win it all
   Zero
   Even, but lacks value
   So why can't nothing mean something?
   Because we stop the world with our thoughts

Life's Court

   Bongo's pound to a familiar beat
   The feat
   The challenge
   Repents
   In the optical vision
   That reflects betrayal and deceit
   However, a new path must meet
   Greeting mountains with a conscious shovel
   Un-programming computerized reactions
   The infractions of an inconsistent reality
   Penned with victorious ink
   I excited when we linked

The Number

   Strapping armor they file in line
   Blood papers stored in ancient time
   Pass decades they advance the court

Proceeded by the Judge
Very footsteps don't budge
Truth's nudge pushing lies off the cliff
Marching posture is stiff
Their cadence shakes the earth
The time has come
The mission is at hand
Inscribed in YAHUSHA's Everlasting Hand
A mighty blow strikes the pins that imprison carnal minds
Rhymes and reasons
Blinds and seasons open to adjust and block
The rays of atmospheric heat
They leak what powers jet
Yet the weather can't affect the flights detestation
A remnant nation
They shifting lies to facts
The pack proclaims what can't be contained
Only obtained, unstained, naming Him that is He
Draining earthly fluids till the river runs dry
Never shall they die, in their mouth is found no lie
This is written is to who it applies

Let Go

Time traveling backward
The reverse state of mind
Held captive by the borders of the status quo
May Mushah's cry echo
Let my people go

On Repeat

History repeats like a leak
That was perceived to be fixed
Draining the life that once was
And what will be again

Something Rare

What is love is all about?
The shadow of sometimes
A doubt in our reality
Figures of growth add up
Into a blossoming oasis
Flowing with patience and care
The trials may seem too hard to bear
Yet pink diamonds are rare
The dare to chart uncharted territory
Cause not all stories being canvased
With that frame in mind

What It Is

One day eye's will see
What mouths' have spoken
What ears have rejected
What was written in a book
What was misinterpreted by the reader
What was unbelievably true
What is distorted by time
What is to come

What was originally penned
What the majority rejects
What makes you hated by all
What other purpose were you born for?

Amnesia

If one could imagine the time before
If one could imagine a time after
Somewhere in-between is true love
Amnesia is a condition in which one's memory is lost
Tossed by what has never been
Only when psychological baggage disappears, then
You've found what you've been searching

Lonely Sequence

Technically a mental malfunction
The time punch into maturity
Working overtime
Line upon line
Making sure lives are in line
More than a symmetrical thinking
Sometimes your mind is the greatest foe
The spirit man has to show, and reign supreme

Superficial Fabrics

Sewn into the popular view
Stitched by superficial fabrics
That's why we got to have it

The census of the majority
The priority is special
The vision is extraterrestrial
Seen in the spiritual confessional
There are many lessons though
Learned by the teachers of their own philosophy

Get On Up

Taking advantage of the opportunities
Twisted with a drugged perception
Connection to the foundation of the mind's default
Placing fault, chasing faults
Dealing lies trying not to get caught
Life has to be sought
Reasons unknown
Crying precipitation with time overdue
Caught up in the blue
More than just a suspended color
He pulls back the cover
From the ashes of all our mess ups, look up
Sarcastic apologizes to the innocent
A standing ovulation to the champions
Who learn through trial
He who wish to change the dial must endure
Young man... young woman... may you soar

Intergalactic Battle

Gravity reverses the due process
Intellectual amnesia

Trauma seizes you
Hypnotic fear
Inducing, seducing, injecting
Seared memory loss
Level two cost
Intergalactic forces battling your northern hemisphere
Light years from the hearts echo
He'll show
Errors through infrared black holes
Space-time
As gravity tries to prevent everything
Including Light, from escaping
The toll to reverse this deposition?
An electromagnetic force that re-positions

Mutual Transmissions

   You acted bravely, and deserve a finish
   You gave it your all
   So no one can diminish
   That growing pains sometimes cause a blemish
   But recognizing them will replenish
   A soul that poured into another cup
   Sometimes the perception is a love transfer will erupt
   Into an oasis of mutual transmissions
   Many may think it wasn't worth the mission
   Listen, stand still as the water crashes on the shore
   You can be sure
   We can be sure
   That the sand was the core
   As situations tore the garment of understanding

Ripped from the fabrics of the heart
Building upon something sinking
A house doesn't crumble
Because of the blueprints of the builders
Nor because of the geometric placement of its pillars
The miss measurements of inches can be foundation killers
You acted bravely, and deserve a finish
Rewind to the beginning of time if this was rented

Until The End

A crafty man makes the antidote a poison
Created to destroy the Chosen
Ya'acub trouble is coming
And will trouble the souls of those bond
By the coming Oppressor and Impersonator
Nothing new under the sun
Thus saith YAHUAH "I have certainly seen
The oppression of My people in Egypt
On that day
Do not fear what you are about to suffer
Be faithful until death
And I will give you the crown of life
And those who wash their garments
in the Blood of the Lamb
Will have right to the Tree of Life"

International Blues

Chimes, vibes, and grooves
The international blues

Infused with the longing of unity
Not glued together by the superficial
More than just tears on a dry tissue
A six-thousand-year-old issue
A trial makes it official
Perseverance has listed you
With those who overcame
The magnetic force fields
Appeals to the Supreme Courts
As the jury reads the verdict
FLASHBACK
The Exalted One slides His pen
With a memorizing elegance
He pauses, "yeah that's a perfect ending"
He continues
Gliding over the perceptions of the status quo
A story without suspense just won't do
A mind bender
Twisting the fabrics of the human capacity
He continues
"The audacity of them to think I'm predictable"
He laughs

Egg Nog

Nodding to the hypnotic potion
Caution
Warning
Parental advisory on beats synthesized
To create incapacitated addicts
Fanatics

Shooting up illuminated toxins
The diagnosis of a disintegrating generation
Truth invasion is descending
The question is
Who side are you defending?

Against The Wall

One may be forced by life's
Vicissitudes and challenges
Into a humiliating circumstance
Operating below or outside one's desired projection of life
But it's there were you will find your destiny

Prepare For The Mountain

If you are a fighter
Don't train for the knockout
Or to go 1 or 2 rounds with faith
Because the moment you give that mountain
Your best right hook, and it looks you square in the eyes
And smiles like, "that's all you got"
You're in trouble
Train for 12 rounds, I call that
The Rumble in the Jungle

Verbal Lynches

Coming out of the trenches
Roping up verbal lynches
Jim Crow standards on heavenly pensions

Flowing left or to the extreme right
They salute at a 45 degree
33 degrees frozen in suspicious intellect
Time capsuled in ignorance
Thaw your salmonella hindrance
Grill your conscious
Bake your conclusions
Fry inverted convictions
Sauteed in false projections
Before you broil
Loyal to the pimp
The intrusions of an optical illusion

A Closed Chapter

Browning leaves
Even vapors evaporate trees
The painting of words mixed
With dull hues and pastels blues
Caressing the mic
A heart guaranteed to lose
Drifting on boats that take thoughts out to sea
"You see?
In the distance, they fade
Nothing more than watercolors on the horizon
O afflicted one, storm-tossed
And not comforted
Feel the depth of My pain
My rejection
When you called and there was no answer
Or protection

Only a section in the chamber
My vast heart
Behold
I make all things new and will wipe
All those tears that will come at the moment
When you remember those nights
That silent dial
As those tears file down your checks
As you stand before Me rejoicing
Joy speaks"

Social Painting

   Paint with words
   Heards follow the listening
   Blistering cold
   The shoulder of natures social curve
   Likes, drugs, the fix
   Affixed on the mirage
   Sabotage minds spinning backwards
   From the western sky view
   An illusion to the pupils
   The phenomenon of the status quo
   Stats that quote
   A fallen people
   An exodus sequel!

Worthy of Death

   Sin is a punishment worthy of death
   A life sentence to thick darkness

The sedative effect regardless of class
For guacamole colored chips
Eat these automatic clips
Drink this glass
Of death
Or
Tear your hollow clothed heart

Near Summer

Flags fly high
They salute
About-face
Knees-up towards domination
The nation of abomination
Racing invisible doctrines
In a room full of paper scholars
Hashtag degree
The pedigree is bowel waste
They can't taste words
Filled with cow manure coming out of the sewer
Vocal pipes stuffed with excrement
Call the prophet
Call the plumber
It's near summer

Sonic Boom

A slight breeze blows over the dust
The Light before the frequency
A Nation's sonic boom

Shock waves created by an object traveling
Through the air faster than the speed of sound
The Truth
Faster than demonic transformers
Electrons, pistons, beginning with our listening
Not heard through the tympanic membrane
Concepts that drum the ear of your brain
Critical speed is known as Mach 7
Supersonic transport
Unlearned and untaught
No longer confound
To the mischievous technological advances
On our northern atmosphere
Suspended above our eyes
Comprised and constructed
Compromised and obstructed justice
In societies institutional infrastructure
Mind shackles with life sentences
Is their subject matter
However, this matter
Atoms and neutrons created an unstoppable force
Causing a sudden change in pressure
Later wrote in a Book
By a heavenly Professor

Poetic Jazz

   Smoother than a sheet of ice
   Like a well time clap
   Equivalent to standing in mirror fixing a collar flap
   Jazz, rhythm, the groove, soothes the nerves

A musical cup of Joe
Hold the creme
Hold the sugar
Straight.... on the rocks
Sliding across the floor out of socks

Freshwater Well

Turning on the faucet of His presence
The approach of a peasant
Covered in One's red DNA
The play is on repeat
Shuffling a broken heart across the floor
It's in pieces
Some are missing
I don't have time to seek them
You're the Mender
Repentance is a prayer suspender
Upwards
A fresh fragrance
Sweeter than honey
The shelter in the storm
Life that reforms
This broken soul

Poetic Destiny

The space shuttle is on the launching pad
At the Space Center
The set-apart Astronauts
All strapped in for liftoff

Butterflies in their stomach
Dispatch chimes in with YAHUAH
He speaks, "I have held My peace for a long time
I have been still and refrained Myself
Now will I cry aloud like a travailing woman
I will destroy and devour at once
Now I shall act"
"10-4," says the Dispatch
"Initiate engines"
He says
"All systems go." Dispatch replies.
"T-Minus hours until lift-off

The Better Things

You deserve the better things in life
Or else you wouldn't be listening to scriptural records
On chords which are password protected
Bass infecting transcribed musical beats
Put that on repeat
It's the science of life
Sampling The Source
DJ'd to perfection
So snap your fingers
Groovy your neck
Only chosen know this two-step

Political Prisoner

Head nodders
Blue and pastels

Light creams
Deemed scratched
Wait, polished and restored
Don't store this in times freezer
Use it in a urgent leisure
Heaven pleasers
Free her
Political wisdom
Indicted on trump up charges
Sounded with no breath
The volume of the lightless
Can't hold her on a people's arrest
Free wisdom
Free purpose
Free the political prisoner
Who defy the modern times

Art Galley

Violins play your sob stories
Taller than Babel's Towers
The silent language of bringing dead flowers
Comprises modern communication
Society racing
Invisible concepts of linguistics
Non-specific destinations
Lukewarm overtones vocalizing a blind picture
With no eyes, or taste, senseless
Mirroring brush
Frames reflect the pandora's box they're boxed in
Auditory sin

Has become the walls best friend
Hung on the hinges of a gullible nail
A picture on sale
Your image is not worth it
To pay attention to your narrow gallery

Beat Traps

Snare drums
Hidden in the worlds instrumentals
The percussion against your soul
Beat traps
Laced with potential
Devastating counter active vocals
From yellow page locals
To an Illuminati focal
What's your price?
Caution at contemplation intersection
I suggest you wear mind protection

Motion of The Sea

Ocean-liners sailing on the hourglass of sandy shores
Losing time until we change directions
Beached by the sunset
No high-tide regrets
Let faith be your sail blowing you to uncharted waters
Where men become truth martyrs
Murdered by hate's assassins
The sweet sound of waves crashing
Ecological balance

Opportunities boat shall float
With water as the talent
Shifts through the raw balance
Where creativity and chance meet
It's just the motion of the sea

Kings to Ships

Slaves to shoe-shining for tips
Spiced with a black rage pepper in our step
Mixed in a pot, not our own
Far from home, staving
It will never be, you will never see
The balance scales of justice
Must this be repeated
The '60s weren't heeded
But the echo lives on
The same old song

Press On

If your family forsakes you
Remember your brother Yusaph
When grief overtakes you
Remember you are not the first
Nor will you be the last
For the rain falls on many rooftops
It is the journey to the top
The destination and the high call of YAH
So take a deep sigh
Even though it was one

In your bosom that betrayed
Don't be afraid
To face the road alone
He will never forsake you
Even if you can't comprehend
YAHUAH shall defend
And show His hand to be with His servant
Be observant, to the shadow of your walk
Cling closer to the Shepherd who whispers when He talks
Leading you in the path for His Namesake
And if no one lends a hand to bare the stake
Press on, for your support is not in man
And if the whole world is against you
You are a one-man army
With YAH on your side
You will slay every giant
So don't fear their great number
It's unbalanced for a reason
So in every season
Credit will be given on high
That by His Name
He used you to defy the odds

Cool Breezes

   A brush paints pastel blues on a canvases
   With transparent views
   A jam session with no rules
   Freedom within the borders of mind
   Is what the painter seeks to find
   Unbind these colors and let them go

Escaping the clutches of the grays
The brush says, "your indignant hand is dead
Wrapped up in dark hues
It's been four days
And you haven't dipped me
In the cool of light blue breezes
Every time you have thoughts
Of a masterpiece, your joints freeze
Let loose creative and let it flow"

Shadow of Death

Yea, though I walk through the valley
Of the shadow of death
I will fear no evil
For thou art with me
Did you catch that?
It's only a shadow and a shadow
Is just a perception of darkness
So you are scared of a shadow?

Ask, Seek, and Knock

In layman's terms
If you ain't hungry for the prize
You'll give up when you ask
If you hear silence
If you have a little energy
You'll seek
And when you don't find, you'll go home
If you have the slightest enthusiasm

You'll knock
And when the door doesn't open
On the first knock
You'll be eliminated for a lack of courage
But if you have endurance
You pictured the scenario
And saw past the door to the prize
And heard the someone resides inside that house
And what that person has is the ability to dig deep
Knows that if he shall be saved
He must endure the coldness winters
The driest droughts
The most vicious enemies and snakes
He must endure until the end
He must knock until the end
He must knock until
Well done

The Ink Faucet

Life is sometimes a poetic drip drop
Like raining thoughts that never stop
Know that silence is in the pen
A metaphor for a calm peace within

Who You Talking To?

"We live in a cold cold world"
Said the stiff winter's night
Then the pen inked a response
"I shall write the wrongs done to the weak

On sheets of tomorrow's bed
My ink is dipped in the red of those
Who thought they would escaped
My gates… Between these blue lines"
Then the winter's night replied
With a bold face lie
"You forget that this is my hemisphere
We live in a cold cold world"
But he forgot that fire awaits him, amain

Word Sails

If words pushed sails
Then propelled these through both ears
Our fears breed tears not just on this page
But mothers in rage and distraught
Her baby boy just got caught by moving steel
Still, we steal our own gravity
Humanity, floating to mental insanity

The Feeling

When you feel like
An island full of people
Don't speak your language
When you feel like no one can relate
Take a trip to countries where the exchange rate
Is to let that go

Majestic Silence

Sometimes the sound of silence
Is so beautiful
Like a sunrise from the darkest night
Even on this fast pace life train
When it's quiet, refrain
From standing near the doors of your comfort zones
The silence won't kill you
So be still

Late Night Visits

I was told this last night by
The Highest, in the late night hour
That time when He sometimes visits my pen
He said, "People are afraid to not be afraid"
Only sounds could articulate my response
Mmm.
I'm the first person
To feel an earthquake after the needle moves
I'm the one closest to the epicenter
So before a poem, a script
A song, a book, a letter or a quote
The shock wave hit the writer's life first
So may we not be afraid of fear
For in YAHUSHA there is safety

Dear King

I know the struggle

THE WILDERNESS

The fighting
The race
The war
The pain
The wounds
The battle
That no one seems to see
Against all odds
You against the world
With no time-outs
Out of breath and weakening knees
It's no way another way to say it
PERSEVERE
We either make it
Or we die in a machine
That gains power off every fallen soldier
Soldier
As they say in the core
When you can't go anymore
You're only at 40%
So on to that distant mountain
Carrying that load thinking
About those after you who need you this day
This hour, this second
You are an elevator and the shoulders
They will stand on
In the power of the Master YAHUSHA
I need you to PERSEVERE

Young Bird

   Trap by the walls as tall as intergalactic skyscrapers
   We labor to get free
   Paying tolls on a highway that loops
   It's on repeat
   Mind interstates
   Color blues and reds
   Democratic Republic
   Beds we lay in
   Blanketed by sheets
   Just covering our temporary frost
   Lost in our mind
   Have you ever heard that sound?
   So profound are thoughts
   Fought in these 12 rounds
   You didn't even know existed
   You didn't even see the cage
   I'm seeking freedom
   May you get free young bird

Rooms Within Rooms

   Everything can't be spoken
   Those deep nooks and crannies
   Which are within rooms within rooms
   So don't sue her for position and your dispensation
   She was beneath you
   So she couldn't listen
   Rooms within rooms within rooms
   She couldn't hear the knock

THE WILDERNESS

The last time a fellow did
She answered the phone
With a fresh newness
Sweet frankincense on floors
The lace of trouble
Dropped her guard like panties
You entered a room matrix
You didn't leave it as you found it
You rounded to cut corners
You inserted mature inceptions
Instead of righteous set-apart affections
Only through the Master
So the moment she thought twice
The moment the high was over
She created another room
And kicked you out of her depth
Her hurt is in that room within rooms
You have to know
It's not just about how to love a woman
How does she need to be loved?
Only the One who created such
A concept can complete it
Sometimes everything can't be spoken
In those rooms
Her soul is within and her mind is there too
Memories and photos of almost
You have the form of her latest motto
It's a layered a poem that only syncs like eclipses
Her vulnerability only comes out on occasions
Like seasons, so be gentle

Invisible Wars

> Sometimes the verbal intensity is a deafening
> The hunger and the fight for something else
> The thunder of a storm which stands
> Before your eyes consist of metaphysical wars
> On the plateau of my brain
> Sounds insane
> Battle hordes in sound horses
> Spears and invisible nemesis
> Wishing to lord
> Over this supernatural production

Perceived Value

> Pedal to the metal
> No elliptic games
> But these hurdles take effect
> The drive
> In sort of elevated tissue
> No time for crying or thoughts of pity
> It's fitting that the fire
> Has invigorated my bones
> Scorching the forest of mediocrity
> I know my value

To All The Soldiers

> Salute to all my soldiers fighting
> From the gutter in the warfare
> I know it's hard

When there are no shares
Dividend
No profits
Wish we could stop
The bleeding from the streets
Where son's heart stop
To the beat of flying drums
Facing dark tunnels on all sides
Besides
You were stemmed in the hottest pressure-cooker
Look there, over the hills and everywhere
YAHUAH can fix this curse
If we dare
To search

Voyager

Riding to a distant place
My feet has yet to touch
Such travel is through uncultured forest
Blazing a path led by the wind
The win is scripted
With past pain of heaven's ink
Link to a drive of a bulldoze smashing walls
The fire behind and within

In The Midst

The fig tree had no idea
It just reached for the sky
The heavens towards the garden

Well rooted it in a trap
So He could free it
From drowning in pain
That's why sometimes there is no rain
So you can know Who controls it

Honor Due

It started with a sad story
Bleeding tears from blue lines
It was an emergency
I got away from the fist
The low blows and suicidal woes
Letters from the soul trying to escape
Escaping impossible stakes
How much more can one take?
Now it's the pen that will travel
Coast to coast
Credit goes to the Master of the Host
In the harvest to get the people
To safety
Blazing with gasoline hands
The One set him on fire
It is an honor

One Way Trip

Interpret signs of my verbal dialect
Foreign in retrospect
By experience of years
Here's the ticket

Pass the fears on the pitch
I'm picketing fences of voices
On herd marching of hurts
Steamrolling blocks on blocks
That block freedom on all invisible sides

Get Free

May the wind of truth blow you to freedom
You behind bars of the mind's prison
Locked up by thoughts
Seeds and kings without rings
Waiting for the finals
Our inheritance is great
No one can match YAHUAH's offer
So even though you are locked up
I understand
But you only a man
If you get free

Customs

Gliding over the ocean blue
If we could be two
I mean one
If we played by supernatural rules
I mean the tools
Which unlock international mind travel

Through Fires

Title shift like high tide
Moved by shadows of pride
But not quite
Please don't easily take the flight
On mistakes or misconceptions
Hopefully I always use the words
As a proper conception
Against inception of the faintness idea
That I let you down
So don't get it just twisted
Do not think I let you down
So easily as words sometime don't quite mix in oil
Let your oath be on a lifetime
In the hottest hot
In winds with speeds 10×10
Keep your smile on permanent
In droughts of pain
Don't misunderstand my projections
My protrusions of just a moment
It has nothing to do with a lifetime
Comparison are only a fraction
Oh a moment oh love
Learn the sermon
When they lay me in a wooden coffins
If the vision were clear
The mornings are harder
Through valleys
Huge mountains
What is stronger than the reaper?

Is how we get through
Love
Past shadows of death
Stronger than our last breath
May you rest in peace & love
Even when understanding
Can't be grabbed
I will never sit back
And hopefully neither will you
Just us 2, now 1

Walking Books

As the living libraries used to say
"You just have to keep on fighting
Crawling and scratching
Latching on to the Anchor"
I look to the sky
He is the Highest in ranking

Poetic Math

Psychedelic motion
Asking for action
On dry mouth motions of frustration
The occasion of life
Twice 34 times more
Hopefully, I can take this math
And mathematics
And You will multiple my efforts
Before my vapor dissipates

Before the hour is late

A Jacket

With tears in her eyes
She rained down her explanations
From the lack of precipitation
From counterparts
Even though she was told
You don't need a coat in the freezing cold
It's time for her kings
To speak otherwise
To carry the load
We have to face home
We have been given the ability
To carry a burden
With divine help
In the One Who fills out cup
To warm her winter nights

Separation

The precision of progress
Towards the inevitable
Focus up
Through opposing forces
Make the changes
The right angles
In the mud I sing
Earning degrees
Which separate me from where I am

To where I'm call to be
Though I fall 7 times
I remember the Word will help me through

Turbulence

Elevation too high
So don't lean
Own your own shadow
Cause on this journey
If you breathe you choke
On your own reasoning
And understandings
You understand me?

Top Surfing

I had to hop on this
I, I know, I know
Just a little fun
When I heard this
I was like
Sounds like surfing on mountaintops
The narrow slots
Called the Way

The Reasons

No accidents
You moved there
You drove there

Even when steps were left
He took you right
You were met conditions
Circumstances and chaos
No accidents
For a reason
For a reason
For a reason
It was an opportunity
Perfectly
Everything happens for a reason

Ascension and Dimension

Wavelengths distance to reach into another dimension
My ascension is measured in closeness
Right there it is oh yeah
Encrypt it in scriptures
Trust to decipher
I must believe in every fiber
Even when earthquakes rocks you to the core
Even when your feet are sore
March to the Promised Land for it sure

The Story So Far

Well the story starts with lost a memory
Like a blur from the youngest memories
They started on Grantham road
Memories of days with my mother are few
For the most part they were pleasant

Mother wasn't always around
But I love my mother
I never understood her condition
I rolled with it
I wish I could get the full story on her life
How her and my dad meet
Sure I'm gonna ask those things
Today though it's about reflection
Pouring out the innermost depths of the soul
Finding areas which lay dormant
I hope to excavate in these mines

They Still Live

I hope you can hear this
They live, the people sleep
They have created an artificial reality
That has reduced the level of conscience
As our vibrations continue to rise
It is an illusion. it is an illusion
I tell you from, the pits of hell
Which they came
All who see this allusion
They try to paint you out as you're insane
They don't want you to see the real enemy
Color is the proxy of their illusion
To make you always think you
Are not equal
When in fact you are more than
They poison the water
The food

The air
Embedding their messages
Images and sounds
Even hand gestures
Evil medicines
That make you sicker and sicker
They make you depressed
Manipulate your emotions
Adjusting your reality
Do not fear them but you must know
You must know that they exist
Because they have distracted you
To put your attention on money
And material goods
So you can never have a connection with the Creator

I Am The Revolution

Oppressed versus the oppressor
Good versus evil
Racism is a product of capitalism
I am a revolutionary
Black hates white
White hates blacks
Black hates black
Fight among each other
Fight for the truth
Die for the truth
More than talking
More than motion
Power

A movement
Death to capitalism
Death to Imperialism
Life to the Truth

Organic

I'm organic matter in a way
Before black was a label and descending ladder
Rewind pass the burden of hoods and drugs
Depictions of systematic institutions
Poisoning our creative production
It's a mere statistic drop pass shots
At goals that hang us
In buildings with segregated sinks
Jim-Crow rinks
Further than cotton fields
Slaves who can't speak foreign tongues
Or read what they wrote
Because they have a dialect from shores
Of the motherland
Ashanti, Aruba and some others than
That vanished like Mali
It's surprising
That we are organic matter

Free Space

Why did the birds sing
Their sunrise song
With a fresh breeze and chirps

Green leaves are fading
Faded north for the winter
Is coming
But just not yet
I'll bet the song will be on repeat
Singing to the soft beat
Of seasons, these are the reasons
The bird sings
Because it can flap its wing
In a free space
Saying
"I'm glad I don't have to pay for space"

Life Support

Why do you do it
The intergalactic battle
Which is between the reflection
Of subconscious matter
Like coma thoughts
On life support
Report signals
That resemble questions mark
With limited answers
But I'm still breathing
It's still hard
It's just a dream
Cause I have given it every ounce
Every drop reigning passion
Bleeding pain, insane
Mountains claimed

To be trespassers
A dream within a dream
Deemed impossible odds
But the baby is due
2 weeks past the date
May the water break
On the dream awaking from this coma
And on to the next level

Turtle Shells

You know what you need
The speed of limits
Are high astronomical pressure
The lesser is where
My current parks keep saying
It's my fault but learned lessons
Are taught in the stadium
It's the hall of shame
The shell of a turtle
Only peeps out when spoken to
Speak when spoken to
In this shell of reflection
Reflecting of my thoughts in the mirror
Of audible echoes
Let go for the need of performance
Just be and see through the shell
That the world is cruel and heartless
Selfish, cold, and bitter
It's winter's night
But this shell is warm

Why The Caged Bird Can't Fly

Nothing stopped it
Trapped behind the walls of doubt
Explaining the excuses
To a chorus of one, "Tomorrow, next week, next month
I'll fly", it said
Caged and clipped
Viscerally living
Surviving
Getting by
Just making it
It repeated
Every day
Praying for help
Yet it was given wings
Yet it was given earth-shattering power
Earth-shaking, bone-rattling, death raising
Disease fleeing, serpent trampling
Life breathing
Supernatural mountain throwing
Power
Power to fly
In the YAH who created the feather
Yet, until the bird decides
Decides that tomorrow is too late
And the next breath isn't promised
And not another second
Not another minute
Not another thought, doubt, or fear
Is going keep it here

Only when the bird decides
That flying on what it can't see
Is worth the risk
Will the cage bird fly?

The Declaration of a Warrior

Closer, march
Closing in on the promise
"It's a landmine!"
"Run!"
"Fire at 9 o'clock, three clicks out
Cover me"
"Hey, Hey, remember
Have I not commanded you
to be strong and courageous?
Do not be afraid or discouraged
For YAHUAH your Alahym
Is with you wherever you go."
"I will not taste death in Him"
"YAHUSHA!"
"Closer, march!"
"Run!"
"I'm hit, I'm hit, ahhh
You're gonna have to go on without me"
"No no we leave nobody behind
I will never leave
Nor forsake you"
"Closer, closer, closer"
"Adese soldier
"Well done, good and faith servant"

The Sound of Giants

Shrouded in mystery
The mightiest of powers
Inked an unfathomable conquest
Lighting split the day
And darkness emerged
Fallen from heaven
Were these beings who
Sought to overthrow Alahym
And the Lamb
And all the Righteous
But they were deluded by their pride
As time ticking
It would be their undoing

Make The Jump

Up against the wall.
Cornered. A visual trap.
And it's this position in which YAH has fashioned.
The caterpillar process.
That sink or swim, do or die. Survive or dive.
This is how champions are made in the valley of decision.
This is how mountains are moved into the sea.
Radical faith. A leap of faith.
Not believing, but knowing. Not thinking, but being.
And you are. You were. You have been.
Fearing the dark tunnel
Which leads to everything you are called to be.
There is no easy way to the land of promise

THE WILDERNESS

That rolled off the Creator's lips.
There are no comfort zones at the table of greatness.
Take note of the seed which must fight it's way to the surface
Pushing against all that weighs it down.
See, I'll show you a mystery.
The illusions which have buried many
In the graveyard of the doubt.
When walking in a forest
Wild beast attack and storms intensify.
It would seem if one was going the wrong way.
For surely it is a sign of a dead end but on the contrary
It signifies that you are closer than ever before.
After a woman goes through the most excruciating pains
Almost touching death, there is
On the sudden, and unexplainable level of joy.
The pain drifts back into the tide.
Pain and joy.
They will dance at the wedding of your victory.
So at that moment, when the opposing forces increase
And discouragement knocks on the front door
And a quick peek out the window
Reveals they have the place surrounded
And you are seemly outnumbered.
Look again.
For YAHUSHA, the Master of Master is a man of war.
Breath Him in
In a deep contemplation of what is about to happen next.
Up against the wall. Cornered.
It's only one way out, you must fight, you must make the jump,
In the strength of the King
Because the battle is already won.

Fly young butterfly, fly.

She Didn't Know

Valued at priceless
Yet she sells her jewels
To the highest bidders
Trying to cop a feel
This is the deal
It's a contract with thoughts of being unworthy
Of wearing the crown of her foremothers
Head down so long
She can't see in front of her
Yet, her belly carried everyone that walks
Standard of excellence
YAHUAH made it so

Fallen

Sigh
When words don't fit
When words don't compute
Heavenly mathematics
Another lost soldier
To the tree of the knowledge
Of good and evil
A mixed drink
Spiked with the poison
They kept losing
Cause they thought
Too much in fact

No relational trust
In the One who they think is a myth
A legend
Or some sort of joke
Lost hope and put it in knowledge
But it can't save
He's foolishness to the foolish
They thought He went to sleep
He's the Shepherd to the sheep
Moving like still waters
Yet, their pride drowns out His whispers
If you're hated and betrayed
For taking that stand when Lucy tries your life
Smile, for it was written
When they fall to the left and to right
Keep straight, for your crown waits
Endure

Girl Lost

  Defined by curves and hips
  Breast thighs and lips
  Walking with the sharpest tongue
  With that razor blade clap back
  When they try to get a number one
  With fries
  But she advertised
  On her daily menu
  An unhealthy diet
  Of social drugs
  Traps for the thirsty

It was all in her eyes
Love deficit disorder
Concrete, bricks, and mortar
Buried in the phantom past is her father
Who was a rolling stone
Stoned off chasing the tail
Cause he was used to being the butt
Now his daughter values the back
A take on the old hamster trick
An attention fix
From a prescription that was never filled
She's didn't know she was much more
Than caramel dripping
Players weren't even worth a glance
Cause royalty pumped through her veins
Daughter of the King of universe
It's ashamed
Yaduhy girl lost

The Promised Land

Ever had a long journey
But the distance wasn't measured in miles but trials?
These are necessary for the next level
So when you have stood the test
And are immovable, unshakable, unwavering
And you spy out His Promise Land
A land full of giants
Great in number and you report back saying
Surely YAHUAH has given us the land
Let's take it at once

THE WILDERNESS

Only at the moment
When giants look like grasshoppers
Are you ready
Ready to enter the land of milk and honey

QUOTES

Walking towards the Promised Land, most of Yashra'al (Israelites) refused to surrender to Alahym. Surrendering sounds like a simple concept, doesn't it? Hold that thought. Imagine everything you've known for years is stripped from you in one day. Your way of life, your income, your comfortability. The sense of security. It's gone. The battle raged in the minds of Yashra'al (Israelites). It's like how a person wants to quit criminal activity but can't. Like when someone is in an abusive relationship but keeps coming back. What about a job where a person is underpaid and undervalued, but won't quit. What makes a person go back? Bills? Money? That's only the surface.

It's easy to become complacent with slavery. This is what makes surrendering so hard. The truth is, the road to freedom is beyond the minds current capacity. There are no points of reference. It's the unknown. If one is hoping for predictability and security, you should go back to Egypt. It's designed this way on purpose. All perfect gifts require trust in the Creator. YAHUAH wanted a better life for His children, and He still does. He saw their slavery and sympathized with their pain. The long hours and heavy burdens. All they had to do was surrender. He wanted to help carry the burdens.

It's like a child who carries a bag that weighs them down. They will try every angle to show that 'they got it'. Until they see for themselves that the weight is unbearable. Sounds a lot like my wilderness experience. Carrying the worries of this life, carrying sin. I had to let that go. We have to let that go and drown out the conflicting noise. Those teachers and motivational speakers who tell us, "believe in yourself. You can carry the weight, just work harder!" False. The journey in the Way is radically different from that ideology. Freedom says we must surrender to the Truth when it stares us in the face. As you read these quotes, I hope you consider dropping all the the weights that weigh you down.

Quote #1

Deception tells you what you're seeing. Truth tells you what you're not seeing.

Quote #2

You can't expect someone to do for you, what you're unwilling to do for yourself.

Quote #3

It's not the knowledge of Alahym that will change you, it's His introduction.

Quote #4

Democracy is a fiction. America is a capitalist corporation, ruled by the 1%. Better yet, some very powerful banking families. The

President is merely the CEO.

Quote #5

Be careful of what people call 'conscious', because you'll be knocked unconscious if you eat the fruit.

Quote #6

Don't be discouraged if you put in 10,000 hours of flight training to prepare for your purpose. It only takes one mistake to crash and burn.

Quote #7

Uproot weeds in the garden of your thoughts, because they will choke out what's planted.

Quote #8

Bitterness is like a cancer that leads to a slow and painful death. The first sign of this disease manifests itself by constant complaining and being cynical about life.

Quote #9

The more you become yourself, in the beautiful uniqueness YAHUAH created within you, the more He can shine through you. Shining to spread a message and show the world a piece of Him. The more you conform to 'religion', the cookie cutter path, the further you drift from reality and Him.

Quote #10

To get to the person you are supposed to be, it will be the hardest thing you've ever done in your life. It will also be the most rewarding.

Quote #11

Sometimes you may look outnumbered, but if YAHUAH is with you, look again.

Quote #12

Solutions 'black' people have heard of before; Rebuild Black Wall Street, protest, financial protest, riot, loot, march, vote, petition, overthrow the government in a revolutionary war. The list goes on. None of the above have ever worked. Even on a physical level, three main things hinder these solutions from being practical. They are legislation, currency, and military. The war is not on the physical plane at all, it's on a spiritual one.

Quote #13

The Promised Land may seem like a thousand miles away, but it's comprised of single steps. So carry the Light (YAHUSHA) through the darkness like a lantern, and enjoy the next step.

Quote #14

The strong delusion plagues the world like aids, yet people are too healthy to believe they're sick.

Quote #15

The day you seek truth for yourself, is the same day you become a revolutionary.

Quote #16

Don't be too bitter to see your own blessings. Acknowledge them daily. A thankful mind breeds peace.

Quote #17

America has never dealt with blood on her hands from the rape, terrorism, and murder committed against the so-called Negros and Indigenous people. Just because it's swept under the rug, doesn't mean the dirt disappeared. Her dirty little secret will be exposed.

Quote #18

Your purpose is written on heavenly tablets. To find it, you must ask the Author who penned it.

Quote #19

You can choke on your own thoughts, understanding, and reasoning if you travel to an altitude that requires trust.

Quote #20

Love is never to busy to iron out wrinkles that are on the surface.

Quote #21

The victim mindset is the cousin of death. Take 100% responsibility.

Quote #22

The American Dream sacrifices money for false freedom. With that false freedom, you become what that dream wants you to be. A slave.

Quote #23

This current life isn't even 1/100,000,000th of treasures in heaven.

Quote #24

Some people are sleeping while they're wide awoke.

Quote #25

Racism is a construction of the capitalist. The weapon of racism divides the oppressed people so "the oppressor" can hide behind these devices. Why do you think the news recycles injustice constantly? We need to fight the real enemy, this is a spiritual war, and only the Truth will expose and destroy their kingdom.

Quote #26

If we break the law in America (or elsewhere), you know there is a possibility that you can go to jail. Why then do people not believe that if you break the laws of heaven, you will not go to jail in the life to come?

Quote #27

The controversy over the last 2000 plus years. Did the Creator of the universe step foot on this planet? Yes indeed!

Quote #28

Since the joy of YAHUAH is your strength, demons will come for exactly that.

Quote #29

War on drugs. War on crime. War on terrorism. War on racism. What do all these have in common? They all try to suck you into a fight against an elusive bogeyman who the Illuminati created. It's all made to distract you from the real enemy, to engage in an endless, fruitless battle. The irony is, the very people who created and recycle this rhetoric are the biggest drug dealers, criminals, and terrorist.

Quote #30

Sometimes we pray more than we listen. Although we have two ears and only one mouth. I reckon we should listen twice as hard as we pray.

Quote #31

You'll never find joy in material things, only in Him who created us with great purpose to be a servant and get joy out of loving Him and our neighbor.

Quote #32

Relationships with people are a direct reflection of your relationship with Alahym. It's the real you. If one is a deceiver, bitter, hateful, wrathful, depressed, unhappy towards themselves and others, it is a reflection of how they feel towards Alahym. This can only be fixed by opening up to Alahym. He will heal you, and your relations with people will reflect that. Draw nigh unto Him, and He will draw nigh unto you.

Quote #33

Deception is usually done silently, that's why those who speak up change history.

Quote #34

You don't have time for fear, sin, lies, illusions, time wasters, dead weight, boxes, jobs that don't push you to the very reason you were born.

QUOTES

Quote #35

Slave ships landed in the Americas over 400 years ago, but most 'blacks' are still on those ships.

Quote #36

Lust, pride, and fear are the top enemies of man. Lust leads to pride, pride leads to fear, and fear leads to judgment, and judgment leads death. This same order occurred in the garden of Eden with Adam and Hauuah (Eve). The opposite of those things is love, humility, and trust. For with these, you may enter the Promised Land.

Quote #37

Trusting the Messiah is sometimes like walking off a cliff where there are no steps. Yet the steps appear with every step. As soon as you remove the fear of not seeing the next step, joy and miracles occur, and you get to see the power of YAHUAH.

Quote #38

Some have become so comfortable eating slop, eating from the pig's pen. Eating things that kill, forgetting the Father gladly prepared the finest feast. The lost tribes have been treated like animals for so long, they've believed it. Spiritual eating anything the enemy feeds them. We are the head and not the tail, a royal priesthood. It's time we come to our senses and return to the Father who is waiting with open arms.

Quote #39

No matter how much man puffs up his chest, and lifts up his chin, he is just dust, and dust he will return.

Quote #40

Giants look like grasshoppers!

Quote #41

The so-called 'Negro' was freed from the bondage of physical slavery, and at the same time shackles were put around his mind.

Quote #42

Being a writer, I've learned that writing things down is a gift from Alahym. The importance of seeing what's invisible come into this realm is priceless. It gives it texture. If you don't write it down, it stays invisible, and you don't know what it looks like.

Quote #43

Drown out the voice that seeks validation from people. Drown it with the Word. Knowing that you're called, declared right, and greatly appreciated by Alahym. The enemy of our souls and man is always searching for the smallest mistake and weakness in your armor. It's done to condemn you. Never subject yourself to it. For if Alahym is for you, who can be against you?

Quote #44

We must accept the greatness the Creator put within us. We must no longer fear it.

Quote #45

Some lose irrevocable minutes chasing paper, but their running after the wrong Tree.

Quote #46

If you really believe something, speak about it in the past tense.

Quote #47

I'm sure Alahym didn't give us life to build another nation's empire.

Quote #48

It's not surprising that we get no justice in this land. It will get worse for the lost tribes before it gets better. So worst until we've tried everything. From praying to trees to ancestors, and anything in-between. Until we realize that only way to get justice is to go to the Judge of the cosmos, YAHUSHA. To return to the Author of our souls in repentance. The One who is entrusted to Judge world. Only then, will He answer us from heaven. Like He did before, when He said, "I have surely seen the affliction of My people who are in Egypt and have heard their cry because of their taskmasters. I know their sufferings, and I have come down to deliver them out of the hand of the Egyptians."

Quote #49

Alahym may set you up for what seems to be an oxymoron. A land with giants in it. A position that's yours but it's already filled. A promise that is not humanly possible. It all comes down to one simple question. Do you believe what He told you? If you do, not one of His words, from generations of eternity's past has ever failed. A stellar record, so what is there to fear?

Quote #50

Yusaph (Joseph) was sold into slavery by his brothers, then to the Midianites, who sold him to the Egyptians. This is likened to the Yashra'al (Israelites) being sold into slavery by their brothers, then to the Africans, who sold them to the Europeans. It's nothing new under the sun.

Quote #51

America. Where you're you can be convicted for a 20-year-old crime, but not the one caught on tape.

Quote #52

Liquor stores, churches, abortion clinic, projects, schools, churches, soul food spots, white Jesus. Poison, poison, and more poison. When are we going to fight? When are we going to sweep behind our own back door? Are we going boycott these schools teaching lies, and these textbook companies?

What about food companies giving the people heart disease and diabetes? Or companies getting paid to kill babies? These poisons have created a mental plantation that the new slave masters profit off of. It's time to escape.

Quote #53

What was the real reason Martin Luther King Jr. was killed? The answer could be found in his last two speeches. He started to shift to economics, via the poor people's campaign. It revealed the next level of the fight. A fight consisting of leaving the burning house he helped integrate the Negro into.

Quote #54

America is like of a playground whose kids are brainwashed to believe they've got the best playground. All until a kid decides to go outside of the sandbox.

Quote #55

Since life and death is in the power of the tongue. The fruit of your life will be the direct result of the words you speak. Ripe or rotten. Make it your agenda, to purposely sow the Word into your life. Speaking life, OUT LOUD everyday.

Quote #56

Alahym will bring the food to the lion, but the lion must be bold enough to pursue, kill, and eat!

Quote #57

Dear Entrepreneur. Alahym should be your CEO. So make sure all executive and creative decisions are approved with Him before you make a decision. The only time we fail is when we forget to acknowledge Him.

Quote #58

It is not enough to read the scripture. A farmer can read the package of seeds daily, but they must be sown. Words are seeds. Words are also pens that sign covenants that lead to a beautiful life of heaven, or an evil life filled with death. Whatever you sow within your mind, you will also reap.

Quote #59

Constant stimulation to violence (and other forms of lawlessness) via technology desensitizes human emotions. Put technology in its proper place. Be sure to always be aware that you 'feel', and never get to use to seeing wickedness. You will become an emotionless robot if not checked.

Quote #60

Guard your eyes and ears because the devil seeks a way into your house.

Quote #61

If a person does not see your value, then you can't force them to see it. Love is not in words but in deeds and action.

Quote #62

Lost tribe men murder each other daily by gang violence, while other nations murder us at the same time. Right there, you have a silent war on both fronts. Divide and conquer at its finest. May Alahym use this atmosphere to awaken His Sheep!

Quote #63

An older man said to me, "what's happening in America with police brutality is nothing new. It hasn't stopped since we got off the boat." Somehow we let the media trick us into believing these crimes were new.

Quote #64

The fig tree struggles, a seed covered by dirt, buried and forgotten. Or is it just process?

Quote #65

It's amazing how a 'hobby', unique as a fingerprint, can be tossed into the trash. Buried in a treasure chest with other gems that the Creator has given to you. It's about stewardship. Imagine if someone gave you something so precious, and your gesture of appreciation is to put it in the trashcan. Isn't that disrespectful?

Quote #66

The founding fathers of the Negro Wall Street of America build a prosperous community, but most of their parents were former slaves. So what's our excuse?

Quote #67

Academic terrorism is defined as the slaughtering of the mind by mis-education and lies. This type of terrorism has this core belief; If you can control the minds of the people, you can control their fate.

Quote #68

Dear America, you can use the media Jedi Mind Trick (misdirection by demonizing the afflicted) all you any want, but I'm still going to talk about what you did.

Quote #69

The devil tries to cover the Truth in feces to keep people away from it. Some treasures need cleansing. In other words, the Messiah's existence and good news can't be defiled by demons. They hate His guts and will try everything to keep them from the Truth. They know it spells doom for them.

Quote #70

Reverse 'racism' is real. As soon as truth hits a person with this spirit, suddenly 'color doesn't matter'. If it doesn't matter, why have Europeans painted all the images like them? Wrote people out of history? Why do the same people who say this, ascribe to these lying images? Truth matters, and because someone sets the record straight, doesn't mean they hate.

Quote #71

Do not neglect yourself or your needs. Sometimes ask yourself. How are you (yourself) doing? How are you feeling? Whatever the answer is, confront it head-on. If you try to bury it, it will only lead to a breakdown. Take care of yourself. Be aware. How can you love your neighbor if don't love yourself?

Quote #72

When the Creator says to love Him with all your might, soul and strength, He means every drip drop.

Quote #73

Just because there is an opportunity to help someone, doesn't make it the will of YAHUAH. Be ok with that.

Quote #74

Inadequate resources is not an excuse to not get started. What did the Word say to Mushah (Moses)? "What is in your hand?"

Quote #75

The moment you believe the Light that seeps through your pores originates from you, you're unplugged from the Source, YAHUAH.

Quote #76

Statistically, jails attract 'black' men. It's like he can't get the memory of the shores of Africa out of his mind. Where they put him in stocks and pins until they could get free labor out of him.

Quote #77

Nothing on earth worth having is more important than YAHUSHA. He is eternal life.

Quote #78

If it comes down to it. Some people will pick a job over the Truth.

Quote #79

YAHUAH will sometimes test you for this simple reason. To see how bad you want it.

Quote #80

True humility is 100% confidence in Alahym.

Quote #81

Everything you need for your dream is already there, down the street of trust. The issue is, you have to walk up that road to see it come to past.

Quote #82

His name was originally YAHUSHA, not Jesus.

Quote #83

Life is like a dance, it's only a couple who find the rhythm.

Quote #84

One day 'black folks' will see that we are powerless without Alahym.

Quote #85

You have to take control of your thoughts and regulate them. Speak shalum (peace) to your mind. Most of all, you have to invite YAHUAH into your thoughts to give you clarity. From small decisions to big ones. He's concerned about you.

Quote #86

Enjoy the experience of life YAHUAH has given us. Our testimony is the only thing we can take with us when we die. Remember where He has brought you from, and how He's used you. Enjoy the experience, not just the destination.

Quote #87

Slavery works like this: you either risk death and escape the plantation or die a slave.

Quote #88

Some men in the world, who're valued so much among men, are an abomination in the sight of Alahym. Why then do men praise them?

Quote #89

Satan doesn't want you to know the authority you've been given in YAHUSHA Messiah.

Quote #90

Sin is like kryptonite.

Quote #91

Artificial Intelligence is trying to replace the spirit of Alahym.

Quote #92

If Alahym showed you how much time you had left, you would move with a lot more precision.

Quote #93

It's funny how Jewish people are quick to make accusations of anti-semitism when they are Europeans. No Europeans were in ancient Yashra'al (Israel). So who is the real descendant of Shem?

Quote #94

Think about the concept of air. It's invisible, yet you need it to live. The Creator is invisible, yet you need Him to live!

Quote #95

When people deny the Messiah, they deny their own breath, their own existence.

Quote #96

Why should you put your all into each moment… because life is only minutes, hours if blessed.

Quote #97

It's a joy to be a thread in the tapestry of YAHUAH.

Quote #98

The subconscious is like a video recorder. Watch what you record.

Quote #99

The new Pharaoh is the dollar. Making you a slave from 9 to 5.

Quote #100

There is punishment for not using the talent Alahym has given you.

Quote #101

It's not He helps those who help themselves. He helps those who have faith to take the first step, because we can not do anything without Him.

Quote #102

If you are not striving, challenging, developing, stretching, and growing to be exactly what Alahym created you to be, then you will die miserably.

Quote #103

When you're dealing with snakes, make no sudden movements.

Quote #104

The darkness doesn't proceed the Light. For it existed before there was darkness, and will be thereafter it's gone.

QUOTES

Quote #105

The most successful counterfeits are those that seem like the real thing.

Quote #106

Don't just focus on learning, unlearning is part of the process too.

Quote #107

It means nothing if your monetarily rich and your soul is still broke.

Quote #108

If you're spiritually is digital, what happens when the power goes out?

Quote #109

Google is the new god to some.

Quote #110

You better believe that the evil spirits that destroyed Black Wall Street never died, they just went to sleep.

Quote #111

The King of the universe going overthrow these wicked governments. Ain't going to be any more Presidents.

Quote #112

I call this, schemes of the devil against 'black folks'. "Anger and insult them until they become irritated and confused. Then, they will act without a plan."

Quote #113

We are the general's of our temple, YAHUAH is the King of the Empire. Acknowledge the King before you enter any war.

Quote #114

A lot of destruction can come if you replace love with pride.

Quote #115

Life is a battle, so learn the art of war. Light vs. Darkness.

Quote #116

We haven't always been slaves.

Quote #117

Don't let age eroded your imagination.

Quote #118

You know you're getting old when you say the exact same thing older folks said to you. Why do you listen to that garbage?

Quote #119

Don't be bound by your own prison, or the one others wish to lock you in.

Quote #120

Covetousness is futile. If you get what's another man's, you're still going to die without it.

Quote #121

If you don't have your lid screwed on tight, someone will hit you with that hocus-pocus and turn you into a goblin.

Quote #122

Some people waiting for the great deception, but they're been deceived already.

Quote #123

Escape the Alcatraz of your mind, the bars of the defeated mentally.

Quote #125

Capitalism is wage slavery. Forcing your cooperation in the weekly Ferris wheel.

Quote #126

Once you figure out how intense the second death is, then you'll discover how intense salvation from it is. Halaluyah for YAHUSHA!

REVELATIONS

"And it came to be, on the third day in the morning, that there were thunders and lightning, and a thick cloud on the mountain. And the voice of a shophar was very strong, and all the people who were in the camp trembled. And Mount Sinai was in smoke, all of it because YAHUAH descended upon it in fire. And its smoke went up like the smoke of a furnace, and all the mountain trembled exceedingly. And when a voice of the sounded long and became very strong, Mushah (Moses) spoke, and Alahym answered him by voice (Sham/Exodus 19:16, 18, 19)."

The introduction of the Word. An unspeakable, fearsome, awesome and mind-boggling event. Can you fathom it? The Creator of the cosmos introduces Himself to His children. All the slavery and sudden freedom built up to this moment. Oftentimes pain is the road to a life-altering revelation. In fact, you can say it's one of the purposes of the wilderness. To officially meet Alahym. He shared His Name, letting them know Who saved them. He gave them His eternal instructions, "to observe all these statutes and to fear YAHUAH our Alahym, that we might always prosper and be preserved, as we are this day (Dabar/Deut 6:24)." It sounds like a love story. Yet, after all these great and mighty sights they saw, YAHUAH's anger would burn against them. The result was a forty-year trip. Wandering until the whole generation, who had done evil in His sight, was wiped out. We must learn from their disobedience.

March 10, 2008, was the day I left Egypt. I then traveled to my Mt. Sinai to meet Him, to receive the revelation of His character, His might, and life's purpose. The currency of the revelations gained in the wilderness is invaluable. The journey from A to B must run its course and all the lessons must be learned. It's definitely not easy. There were many times, when I looked at my watch, impatiently hoping that His deliverance came at any moment. Walking through the terrible wilderness with snakes and all kinds of elements, you realize that some of the most beautiful gems wouldn't be found if you went another route. While you read these revelations, may you value the intangible treasures you've been giving, because they are more precious than gold.

THE EARTH

Mother Earth

Observing works of YAHUAH, you can see His patterns. Look at the sun, moon, and stars. All spheres. Now, look at a human egg covered in sperm under an electron microscope. It's a sphere. The sperm even looks like little people on the earth! All sperm die, and only *one* went inside the egg (earth) to bring life! Does that sound like a parable? Think about it, Adam came out of the egg or sphere, i.e. earth!.We all start as eggs, which are like a mini earth. Also, a sphere is 360 degrees in all directions, which is infinite. This pattern bares witness of Alahym. It's a pattern! It ain't called 'mother' earth for nothing.

The Center of The Universe

One day I was in deep thought and pondered, "why would YAHUSHA come to this little ole earth?" After all, there are billions upon billions of galaxies in the universe. Some scientists say it could be up to 500 billion galaxies. My estimation is its way more than that. His creation is unfathomable. Praise be to YAHUAH, the Maker of the heavens and earth! Inside those galaxies are billions and billions of stars and planets. Yet, the earth has the attention of the Creator? Not long after I asked this question, the answers started coming. There is new scientific data that challenges the Copernican Principle. A principle created by scientist Nicolaus Copernicus, who believed that the earth wasn't in any particularly privileged position in the solar system.[10] Evidence against this theory is substantial. Many test and surveys show that the position of the earth wasn't only placed perfectly in the solar system, but the universe too. One of the greatest tests was the Sloan Digital Sky Survey and the Planck satellite data.[11] The results revealed that the Milky Way galaxy is in the center of the known universe. I'm a big believer in the patterns of YAHUAH. Looking at ancient maps of the earth, you can see Yarushalayim (Jerusalem) at the center of the world. Could it be that the earth is at the center of the universe? The earth is more significant than what we thought!

HOW AMERICA BECAME GREAT

Stocks and Bondage

In history class, they never taught us that some of today's top enterprises became profitable because of the transatlantic slave trade. This trade was rooted in the New York Stock Exchange. The Buttonwood Agreement, which started what became the New York Stock Exchange, was signed in 1792 under a buttonwood tree in front of 68 Wall Street.[12] This is about a block away from the slave market at the intersection of Wall and Water streets. The agreement covered transactions and companies involved in the slave trade, including shipping, insurance, and cotton.[13] With a free slave labor force, America quickly rose to the top. Fast forward to today, so-called 'minorities' make up the majority of poverty-wage work. In 2017, our average household income was median income for an African American household was $39,490 compared to $68,145 for Europeans. Asians came in at 81,331, and Hispanics rounded out at 50,486. [14] With those numbers you can understand that slavery was never abolished, it transitioned to a new frontier. In the end, the first will be last, and the last first.

MIND WARS

MK-Ultra

Desensitization. You can only see murder, violence, and innocent blood being spilled so many times before you become desensitized to it. Through the media, Satan is using a military tactic called MK-Ultra.[15] The goal is to constantly expose people to violence and brutality while creating an insensitivity to it. People then become out of touch with reality. An innocent person gets their head blown off and it's, "It's just another Nigger." This opens the door for more executions with no resistance. Human loss of life is devalued. Think about it, if people can't get a conviction against a murderer for killing a person on camera, what's stopping them for killing masses of people with no repercussions? This progression is what will cause people to be beheaded for the witness of YAHUSHA according to Rev 20:4! It's a war for your minds.

The next goal by Satan is to take your mind, will, emotions, then your soul. MK-Ultra is the vehicle. You see this when so-called 'blacks' have great civil right victories, but it's quickly followed up by a subliminal importation. Which says, "Negro, you can only go this far, if you go past here, we'll check you." An MK-Ultra secret psychology warfare trick used by the media. It produces a spirit of brokenness. Once hope is gone, the will to fight back goes with it. Those who do fight back are silenced. MK-Ultra is an age-old weapon that the slave masters used. How can you have 50 slaves and 4 Europeans on a plantation, yet the slaves fear a rebellion?

Don't forget Operation Paperclip. A government program where over 1,500 German scientists from Adolf Hitler's Nazi Germany were employed to the United States after World War II.[16] MK-Ultra brainwashing is real. We can't fall victim to it. While the world becomes heartless and cold due to this trick, we become burning torches of love.

DREAM OF BABYLON

Babylon Will Burn

In a classroom, there was Yashra'al (Israel) and believers from all different nations. The Teacher played a videotape of all the evil and wicked things Babylon The Great Whore did over the years to the children of YAHUAH. All the bloodshed, all the times they got away, and no one could render justice for them. I remember being so sad, but sadness turned into anger. Then the Teacher turned the tape off and said, "The flame that is YAHUSHA's eyes when He comes is His fury." The day of YAHUAH will be a day of gloom. Never will there be a day like it. It's filled with vengeance, and that day burns like an oven. His love and kindness is now open for repentance, but He has recorded everything the world has done!

THE WORD

Every Knee Will Bow

YAHUSHA is highly exalted. One with the Father, and able to receive worship, honor, and praise. Be reminded, mankind has never dealt with the Father directly, only His Son. The Word and the Voice of YAHUAH, His Right Arm, since the beginning. In the beginning, Alahym, Aleph and Tau (Beginning and End) created the heavens and the earth. From Adam to the Patriarchs, to the Prophets, and Kings, they all dealt with YAHUSHA. Everything in the universe will worship the One who sits on the throne and the Lamb! He is the representative of the Father's Kingdom. "Worthy is the Lamb having been slain to receive power and riches and wisdom, and strength and respect and esteem and blessing (Haz/Rev 5:12)!" Don't believe anyone who tries to put YAHUSHA the Master down, for He is highly exalted! Since He is this great, how great is our Father? We can't even comprehend!

He Will Be Who He Will Be

He will be in a Burning Bush. A Pillar of Fire. A Guiding Cloud. An Army General. An Anonymous Messenger who won't say His Name. Fire on a mountain, and so big, all you see is the bottom of His foot. All you can see is His back. A Mighty Wrestler who will cripple you. A Mysterious Figure saving people from scorching hot furnaces. The appearance of a Gardener, so you thought. A Stranger who sparked a conversation to see what you knew, then vanished before your eyes. He will be who He will be. This is the Son of Alahym the Father, YAHUSHA, He is YAHUAH (I Am That I Am).

A Shadow of Things To Come

Yusaph (Joseph) was sold into slavery by his brothers. In fact, Yahudah (Judah/Judas) betrayed him for 20 pieces of silver and sold him to a foreign nation. Before Yusaph (Joseph) went into the pit, they stripped him of his robe. He went to prison for a crime he didn't commit. Then in Egypt, Potiphar appointed Yusaph (Joseph) over his whole house. No one was greater than Yusaph (Joseph) in Potiphar house. All that he had, he gave into Yusaph (Joseph) hand, and YAHUAH blessed his house. Who does this sound like? For Yusaph (Joseph) life was a shadow of YAHUSHA's life. For YAHUSHA was betrayed by his own, Yahudah (Judah/Judas) for silver, sold to another nation, stripped of his robe, and charged with a crime He didn't commit. He arose from the tomb with all power in heaven and earth! No one in the universe was greater than Him other than the Father. Esteem to the Alahym the Father for YAHUSHA!

Infinity and Beyond

The infinite Alahym the Father, existed in the timeless pass, having no beginning. The universe itself, which is infinite, is likened to a canvas in which He existed in before anything was. He Himself, on the throne. He brought forth the Alaph and Tau (Beginning and End), the Word, to speak, to fill this canvas of infinity. Which, in theory, is mind-boggling, for how can infinity be filled? Is there no end to space as we know it?

He created man and the first commandment was, "Be fruitful and multiply and fill the earth and subdue it (Bar/Gen 1:28)." Is this a parable? Surely YAHUSHA filled the universe with the esteem of YAHUAH. "For by Him, all things were created, in heaven and on earth, visible and invisible, whether thrones or dominions or rulers or authorities—all things were created through Him and for Him (Qol/Col 1:16)." These are only thoughts, for we only know in part. One thing I do know is, oh how great is His majesty! YAHUAH works are unsearchable!

The Bread of Heaven

Alahym commanded the clouds to open and manna, known as the Bread of Heaven, fell to the ground in abundance. It was the food of Messengers (Angels). This was more proof to Yashra'al (Israelites) that no barrier or location could hinder the Alahym's provision. That's love. It was a miraculous event meant to teach them Dabarim 8:3 (Deuteronomy). Where it is written, "Man shall not live by bread alone, but by every word that comes from the mouth of Alahym." What does that really mean? Tahillim 78:23-24 (Psalms) gives us one answer, "He commanded the skies above and opened the doors of heaven, and he rained down on them manna to eat..." Did you see it? Alahym commanded. He spoke a word and gave orders to the clouds. Their provision was based upon the Word. The Word of the Father, who is the Son of Alahym.

Yashra'al (Israelite) failed this test because they put their trust in who they could see, Mushah (Moses) and Aarun (Aaron). Yashra'al (Israelites) said to them, "If only we had died by the YAHUAH's hand in Egypt! There we sat around pots of meat and ate all the food we wanted, but you have brought us out into this desert to starve this entire assembly to death (Sham/Exod 16:3)." Yashra'al (Israelites) choice of words against Mushah (Moses) and Aarun (Aaron) is striking, "you have brought us out..." Yet, it was Alahym who brought them out. The predictability of slavery became so ingrained within their subconscious that only a supernatural transformation could fix it. The truth of this has not changed. Trusting the Word completely is sometimes like walking off a ledge with no visible steps, but with each stride, steps appear. This is a crucial lesson in the wilderness. Without it, you will miss the daily miracle manna Alahym provides.

HEAVENLY EQUATIONS

The Ladder

The Word of spoke from the mind of Alahym the Father in the beginning (Bar/Gen 1:1). This Word exists, in its current state, in the past, present, and future (Haz/Rev 1:8). This Word, not only has the edict of the totality of the universe and time, (Yasha/Isaiah 46:10) but the purpose of each and every righteous citizen (Eph 2:10). A Word finished after it was spoken. Spoken in the Abry (Hebrew) tongue through the Master. He formed and took the Ruach (Spirit) of each Abry (Hebrew) letter, and it turned into a mathematical equation. These mathematical equations formed a spectrum of light, this light is color. These colors are not on a human color wheel. Colors connected to the temple (body) of the Righteous Ones. More specifically, these lights and colors come from heaven. They're connected to the set-apart of set-apart place located in the mind of the Righteous One. This beam of incredible, intense, and indescribable color is Ya'acub's (Jacob's) ladder. Ya'acub (Jacob) saw Messengers (Angels) ascending and descending on the ladder, on the mount Batyh Al (House of Al). The same mount where the temple would stand. The temple in Yarushalayim (Jerusalem) was a shadow of what is in heaven. Our body has the same pattern of that temple. We are temples. What does this ladder of light and color look like? A DNA helix! Ya'acub (Jacob) saw a DNA helix structure! The Abry (Hebrew) word ladder is "sullam" which means a staircase. Now look at the DNA helix, and see how it is a staircase. Not only that, let's look into a DNA helix. The amount of information in a pen head of DNA is enough information to reach the moon a couple of times. [17] Also, in a DNA helix, there are little proteins called enzymes to go up and down the DNA strand. They work, delivering messages from the brain, looking for errors and making repairs. [18] Enzymes do their work on a minute by minute, second by second bases. What does this sound like?! Ya'acub (Jacob) said he saw messengers ascending and descending from heaven! Messengers (Angels) deliver prayers and answers for the righteous ones according to the Scriptures! Messengers (Angles) are like the enzymes, going up and down the ladder from heaven to the earth.

It is up to us to send vibrations to heaven through the Ruach ha Qdush (Set Apart Spirit). Everything that exists has a vibrational frequency, all matter, even solids. Vibrations produce frequencies. Why does this matter? The spiritual world is based on vibrational frequencies. Prayer, worship, praise, and commands. Sometimes in the spiritual world, the vibrational frequencies are high because of demonic warfare. Demons attempt to stand in the midst of your Ya'acub's (Jacob's) ladder, slash the spiritual DNA helix, slash spectrum of color. If successful, it can prevent righteous Messengers (Angels) who are sent to deliver your prayers from you (up), or answers to you (down). The book of Dan'al (Daniel) is a prime example of this. If anything was in the midst of a DNA helix, it is a malfunction or virus. Now you can see why some prayers take much force and even fasting because your vibrational frequency must be raised. Raised to such a height that it will move YAHUAH to act, to send help from His Set-Apart Place. Once the sounds of these vibrations create a frequency that cannot be hindered by opposing forces, a rhythm is created, a sweet smelling fragrance to YAHUAH.

SHINE BRIGHT

Shine The Light

"You are the light of the world. A city set on a hill cannot be hidden; Neither do people light a lamp and put it under a basket. Instead, they set it on a lampstand, and it gives light to everyone in the house. In the same way, let your light shine before men, that they may see your good deeds and glorify your Father in heaven (Matt 5:14-16)." There were three places where the light should shine. We are the light of the world, the light of the city, and the light of the house. In other words, let our light shine in your house, in your city, and in the world!

HEAVENLY BOOKS

Everything Is Written

There are heavenly books, which detail all the days of our lives in vivid description. "Your eyes saw my unformed body. And in Your book all of them were written, The days they were formed, While none was among them (Tahill/Psalms 136:16)." To think, our heavenly Father and His son thought about, then map out those days is breathtaking and empowering. Blessed are those who decide to seek Him and His kingdom, design, plan, and map for our lives. Others spend their life in vanity, trying to 'control' their destiny. Blessed are the ones, who have given up their lives to gain a new and better one. Better than what they could ever plan for themselves. Remember, Alahym has the blueprint for your life, so why do you need one? You have to learn what is already written in His scroll about you! Ask, seek, knock to Him with a pure being, and He will peel back the layers in that book. It will blow your mind!

CLEAN vs. UNCLEAN

The Schoolmaster

I always wondered why the Turah (Torah) was so strict when it came to *clean vs. unclean* matters. Let's say an unclean thing touched a wooden article, clothing, utensils, skin, or a sack; The other article was made unclean. Even ovens or pots were destroyed because something unclean touched it. This was a shadow of how we are to live our lives. Think about this. If something was poisonous in your sandwich, so poisonous it would kill you, would you try to find the poisonous part, cut it off, and eat the rest? Or would you throw it away because it's too risky? Why would you risk your life over a sandwich? The Word of YAHUAH was showing us the relationship we are to have towards sin. The areas of our lives are pots, ovens, and articles of things. If something unclean touches it, it must be either washed or destroyed. There is no compromise. There is no, "well let me just cut the bad part off, and eat the rest" (<— guilty of). Remember, sin will kill you. "For the wages of sin is death, but the gift of Alahym is eternal life through YAHUSHA our Master (Rom 6:23)."

DECEPTION

Like A Video Game

Stages are being set for deceptions that are greater than our senses can even process. In fact, the day is coming and now is here where you can't trust your eyes or hears. If possible, these deceptions would deceive the very Elect. Deception is elusive, sometimes impossible to detect. We have to weigh opposing facts on a scale called discernment. Those red flags and gut intuitions are crossroads to rethink, reevaluate, and reprocess. Please, when you come to this fork in the road, take all the time you need to see what direction you should go. "And lean not on your own understanding; Know Him in all your ways, and He makes all your paths straight. If not, "he who hurries with his feet sins (Mash/Pro 3:5-6, 19:2)." YAHUAH will speak with a soft whisper if your emotional music is not too loud. Put on your spirit filled glasses to see through the deception.

WISDOM

Born Again

Chakhmah (Wisdom) is the Mother of the Righteous. Chakhmah (Wisdom) is the feminine power of YAHUAH, a Mother. Look at the word broken down in the Abry (Hebrew).
- Chat — Wall, fence, separation
- Kaf — Palm of a hand, too open
- Mam — Water, womb
- Hay — Behold

Do you see the pattern? The amniotic sac in a mother 'separates' a baby from the outside. The 'hand' of Alahym 'opens' it, and 'water' comes forth, like when people say, "Her water broke." After her water breaks, you will 'behold' a child! "YAHUSHA answered and said to him, "Truly, truly, I say to you, unless one is born from above, he is unable to see the reign of Alahym." Nakdimon said to Him, "How is a man able to be born when he is old? Is he able to enter into his mother's womb a second time and be born?" YAHUSHA answered, "Truly, truly, I say to you, unless one is born of water and the Spirit, he is unable to enter into the reign of Alahym. "That which has been born of the flesh is flesh, and that which has been born of the Spirit is spirit (Yahu/John 3:3-6)."

MONEY

Money Is Not Power

How many times have we heard the phrase, *money is power?* Recently, YAHUAH broke down what you are really saying when you say that. When you do the etymology on the word 'money' and you will come to the word 'Moneta'. This word was originally a title of the Roman goddess called Juno Moneta.[19] Juno Moneta, in Roman mythology, was the wife of Jupiter and was considered the Queen of Gods, and the most powerful goddess. Sounds like the Queen of Heaven mentioned in Scriptures! It's interesting that Juno Moneta image is the same image of the Statue of Liberty. Babylon the Great Whore is another name for her. So if you say "money (Moneta) is power", you are saying Juno Moneta, Babylon the Great Whore, so-called the Queen of Heaven is power.

SLEEP & DEATH

Twin Cities

People don't believe in the resurrection, yet you went to sleep and woke up this morning (hopefully). A mini-resurrection. A daily witness of what YAHUSHA did. Furthermore, whatever you feed your subconscious while you are awake, will rule over you in your sleep. In order words, what you feed yourself while you were living, will rule over you in death, be that good or evil.

THE ISRAELITES

Salvation By Works?

Yashra'al (Israel) was scattered to the four corners for not keeping the Turah (Torah). More specifically, Yashra'al (Israel) was scattered to the four corners for rejecting the Author of the Turah (Torah), the Living Word, who became Flesh. There is a difference. If someone focuses on the letter of the Turah (Torah), you will miss Who wrote it. If you were reading a book, you would first make sure it's from a trusted source. "For YAHUSHA said, "you search the scriptures thinking you have eternal life in them, but they bear witness of Me (Yahu/John 5:39)." The Source of Life and salvation or a self-righteous hypocrite. An eternal commitment through His Son or outer darkness. These are the choices.

SELF-RIGHTEOUSNESS

You Played Yourself

"And behold, one having come to Him said, "Teacher, what good *thing* shall I do that I might have eternal life?" And He said to him, "Why do you ask Me about what is good? Only One is good. But if you desire to enter into life, keep the commandments." He says to Him, "Which?" And YAHUSHA said, "You shall not murder, you shall not commit adultery, you shall not steal, you shall not bear false witness, honor your father and mother, and love your neighbor as yourself." The young man says to him, "All these things I have kept. What do I still lack?" YAHUSHA told him, "If you want to be perfect, go, sell your possessions and give to the poor, and you will have treasure in heaven. Then come, follow Me." And having heard this statement, the young man went away grieving; for he was *one* having many possessions (Matt 19:16-22)."

For years, I never caught it. The first sentence, "what good thing shall I do," pause. His first words began with an assumption that he could do something to "have eternal life." His grave error was self-righteousness. "For it is by loving-kindness (grace) you have been saved through faith, and this not from yourselves; it is the gift of Alahym, not as a result of works, so that no one may boast (Ephes 2:8-9)." He erred because he thought he had the power to save himself. He had been doing things in his own power and not trusting Alahym. So when the Master said, "if you desire to enter into life, keep the commandments", he should have said, "Master, I can't keep the commandments without you. For I can do nothing without you."

TEACHERS

Whitewashed

I had a dream of a long white table that looks like a feast was about to begin. A man at the table was brown-skinned, and had a turban on with an all-white garment on. At the table, a person brought out a silver platter. When they opened it, it was two roasted pigs on it. He put salt and pepper on them and was about to eat. It also seemed as if he was waiting for others to arrive. The interpretation of this dream is this. There is a so-called leader in the Yashra'al (Israel) community who is laying abominations before the people with little to no effort. This abomination is self-righteousness.

THE KINGDOM

Not of This World

"But seek first the reign of Alahym, and His righteousness, and all these shall be added to you (Matt 6:33)." YAHUSHA once told the people "The Kingdom of Alahym is in your midst (Luk 17:21)." Don't confuse the Kingdom of Alahym with a physical kingdom, but rather the authority for YAHUSHA to rule in His Father's kingdom. To seek and crave for the Kingdom of Alahym, is to desire the eternal and everlasting rule of YAHUSHA on earth. Seek His righteousness, that is, the Turah (Torah), the Word, the Way. Seek the Son to find the Father, and when you find Him, and you will be His child forever. Crave first, the eternal will rule of YAHUAH, and His Righteousness (the Word)!

PRIDE

It's Levels To It

"My power and the strength of my hand have made for me this wealth! (Dabar/Deut 8:17)." A statement of pride. Pride comes before the fall. Many motivational speakers of today bait people into this trap. "The strength of my hand" sounds a lot like, "my hard work got me here." Very dangerous words. I've learned that it's levels to becoming humble on this journey through the wilderness. Let's go from pride to humility.
1. Prideful — "I've built this with my own hands."
2. Still Prideful — "Alahym, tell me what my purpose is so I can do it."
3. Humility — "Alahym, I need your help, please direct my

path because I cannot do nothing without you."

SPIRITUAL TIME

Time Is Short

YAHUAH sits outside of time. All moments in time (bound by the elements of the universe) and motion are moments He can look at. Think about the Creator looking into a fishbowl. This fishbowl that has all the moments that will ever exist. All moments are, and exist. Everything is written, yet, the motion of time is still moving towards future moments. Now think about that fish in the fishbowl. It could swim to a territory in water, but it would take time. The geographical location of the water the fish is traveling to exist whether the fish swims to it or not. The earth is like this fish. Earth is fundamentally traveling through the fishbowl to a certain territory. There is a territory, a geographical location where a moment exists, yet the earth takes some time to travel to it. It's a moment where the One who created everything will step through space-time, and intersect with earth time. Picture the fishbowl, let's say it's a huge fishbowl. The Creator of the fishbowl could come into the bowl at any moment in the history of time. It so happens, that YAHUSHA shall come to earth when the earth has reached a certain time. Heaven will then collide with earth at that moment. "Beloved, do not let this one thing escape your notice: With YAHUAH a day is like a thousand years, and a thousand years are like a day (2 3:8 Kapha/Peter)." 7,000 years is likened to 7 days. Ponder now, how 500 years ago is actually only a couple years ago to YAHUAH! Generational sufferings and punishments that last for centuries are really short periods of time. We are sometimes chastised by YAHUAH for only seconds or minutes in His eyes, but to us, it's years.

- 1000 years = 1 day
- 1000 years = 24 hours
- 500 years = 12 hours
- 250 years = 6 hours
- 125 years = 3 hours
- 62.5 years = 90 minutes
- 31.25 years = 45 minutes
- 15.625 years = 22.5 minutes
- 7.8125 years = 11.25 minutes

By the looks of this, we don't have time to waste, not even a second. Tomorrow isn't promised. Life is a vapor. What would you do if you only had 3 hours to live? Would you be concerned with the things you are concerned with now? Would you go to your job? Would you be in that relationship? Once you shift your mind to spiritual time and trust YAHUSHA, life will never be the same. This explains why YAHUSHA spoke with so much urgency, because to Him, He was coming to reign on the earth in a few days! Now that time is even shorter. We should wake up every morning thanking Alahym for the minutes He gives us. Thinking about the spiritual clock, because unless the Messiah is coming back in our lifetime, we will leave this body. What are you going to do with your minutes or hours?

WARFARE

"And they reported to him and said, "We went to the land where you sent us. And truly, it flows with milk and honey, and this is its fruit. But the people who dwell in the land are strong, and the cities are walled, very great. And we saw the descendants of Anaq there too." And Kalab (Caleb) silenced the people before Mushah (Moses), and said, "Let us go up at once and take possession, for we are certainly able to overcome it." But the men who had gone up with him said, "We are not able to go up against the people, for they are stronger than we (Bami/Num 13:27-28, 30-31)." Here were the two schools of thought. Radical trust or cowardly doubt. The difference between them is life and death.

After returning from spying out the Promised Land, most Yashra'al (Israelites) were intimidated by the people who occupied it. The descendants of Anaq were known giants, and I'm sure it was a lot of them. Often times YAHUAH will gut check us. You know, bring us to a moment where we're faced with a challenge beyond our ability. At that moment, fear or trust will be our choices. In this case, the majority of Yashra'al (Israelites) chose fear. Yahusha Ban Nun (Joshua) and Kalab (Caleb) chose to trust in the One who defeated Pharaoh with dreadful plagues. A race of giants would be nothing for Him. Hence, Kalab (Caleb) said to the people, "Let us go up at once and take possession." That's what you call standing firm on the Word. They understood Alahym was greater than any fear. Boldness. Complete confidence not in themselves, but in the Creator.

Walking by faith (trust) and not by sight. Kalab (Caleb) wasn't intimidated by what he saw. The giants. He knew what they were promised by the Word. The way the warrior Kalab (Caleb) reacted is the key to unlocking the door to the Promised Land. Let's break it down. If you read the *Life Lessons on Faith*, you know that it is more than just 'believing'. It's a trust that is unmovable, fully pursued and fixed. We can see this type of trust in Yahusha (Joshua). He was so confident in the Creator, that he asked Him to stop the sun. What great faith! He saw YAHUAH split the sea with ease, and descend on the mountain in fire as it shook. Yahusha (Joshua) knew YAHUAH was all mighty, awesome, majestic, all-knowing, and all-powerful. Nothing is too hard for Him. He knows the number of all the sand grains on earth. He knows all the stars by name. Yahusha (Joshua) had so much trust in Alahym, that he asked Him something so impossible, so staggering, that I can't help but believe that the Father smiled at His Son when Yahusha (Joshua) asked that. To enter the Promised Land, you must be the same way. Fearless. Fearless against any generational curses, demons, sins, people or situations. These will likely be your giants. The way to the Promised Land goes down the street of high-level spiritual warfare. Sorry to break the news to you, it's no other route. Fret not, warfare will only make you stronger. During my journey, YAHUSHA taught me how to war.

How do you fight? It's a two-part formula. Throughout the book, we've talked about complete trust. The next part is equally important. Take another look at what Kalab (Caleb) said, "Let us go up at once and take possession…" Did you see it? He took up the authority they had been given! Kalab (Caleb) confidently reacted. The Word had previously given them surety that they would conquer their enemies, then the opportunity manifested itself. In the wilderness, I've learned that one of the greatest tricks of the enemy is to distract you from realizing your authority in YAHUSHA Messiah. YAHUSHA said in Luke 10:19, "Behold, I have given you the authority to tread on serpents and scorpions, and over all the power of the enemy, and nothing will injure you." Read that again. "…over all the power of the enemy." Halaluyah!

Sometimes people are quick to say, "the devil did it" when in fact they did it. Could it be they haven't possessed the authority they've been given? Layers upon layers of generational curses have taught the oppressed to settle for brokenness. From the sin-infested condition of the oppressed and poor, to slaving for a dollar. "It's just how it is. We have to deal with it. Nobody can be perfect anyway." All excuses. No no no. We are called to be whole and excellent. The Word says, "you shall be set-apart, for I Am set-apart (Way/Lev 11:45)." Where are the Kalab's (Caleb's) and Yahusha's (Joshua's) on earth, who look at their lives and say, "no." No, my life is not matching up to what is written in the ancient scrolls, so I'm going to fight. They look at the state of our broken families, communities, and spiritual society and say no. No, I don't care what it looks like, because I know the Creator is greater. Get up from that slop pin young man, young women. Where are the warriors who talk like Kalab (Caleb) when they see a race of giants? These are the people Alahym is recruiting. To be representatives for His Kingdom. People who know His power, and trust and obey Him with all their heart. People who love Him and their neighbor to the point that they will risk their lives. People who have had enough of sin and death, and want to be the change.

The formula thus far is complete <u>Trust in YAHUSHA + Authority = Victory</u>. We should talk more about authority. Early 2018 began what I like to call, spiritual boot camp. Intense is a good word for it. I always knew demons were real, even encountered some back in the day. Yet, I never understood the inner workings of the spiritual world. We won't dive too deep, but what you must understand is that the spiritual world consists of two empires. The Kingdom of Light and the Kingdom of Darkness. YAHUSHA vs. Satan. Good vs. Evil. Light vs. Darkness. Even though there are two Kingdoms, YAHUAH Kingdom reigns supreme with easy. The earth was given to Adam, and he gave it Satan. It's like a legal deed of land that was transferred to another owner. Since then, the Kingdom of Darkness has spread to the ends of the earth. Ultimately, the evil empire is merely a pawn to manifest the greatness of YAHUAH. Evil seeks souls to carry off to everlasting punishment. Here is where it gets deep. The Kingdom of YAHUAH is like a legal system. The Judge is the Son of Alahym. Satan is the head prosecutor. Demons are also prosecutors with different ranks. We see this in the book of Yub (Job). "And the day came to be that the sons of Alahym came to present themselves before YAHUAH, and Satan also came among them. And YAHUAH said to Satan, "Have you considered My servant Yub (Job), there is none like him on the earth, a perfect and straight man, one who fears Alahym and turns aside from evil?" And Satan answered YAHUAH and said, "Is Yub (Job) fearing Alahym for naught (Yub/Job 1:6, 8-9)?" Here you see Satan making an accusation against Yub (Job). Later we read the Judge, YAHUSHA, grants Satan's petition but sets the perimeters. Think about an earthly court, if you were a prosecutor, you would have to go to a judge to sign off on a warrant to make an arrest. See how this works?

Now bring sin into the picture. Sin gives a legal right for demons and Satan to steal, kill, or destroy. It's like a spiritual door. A door that gives them the right to oppress, dwell, and even possess a person. A people's body is a house where a soul and spirit lives. Demons are seeking to enter a person's house, then invite other demons. The goal is to control a person's soul. In other words, to control their mind, will, and emotions. The first step for demons is to persuade a person to sin. If successful, they have evidence go to the Judge and petition for the rights to steal, kill, destroy. Along with that, is the right to oppress or even possess a person. Oftentimes, like in the case of Yub (Job), Satan will persecute the righteous because he wants to see them destroyed. In all cases, the Judge will determine what will be the righteous judgment. Understanding this dichotomy gives a new meaning to Ekah 3:38 (Lamentations), "Do not the evils and the good come out of the mouth of the Most High?" Let me get this straight. According to the Word, the Devil can not make you sin. Remember what YAHUAH told Cain? "If you do what is right, will you not be accepted? But if you refuse to do what is right, sin is crouching at your door; you are its object of desire, but you must master it (Bara/Gen 4:7)." It's a choice. Life or death. Cain was persuaded by Satan and gave in to that desire. "The wages of sin is death, but the gift of Alahym is eternal life (Rom 6:23)." This means that spiritual warfare comes down to two choices. We are in the midst of a spiritual legal battle for souls. YAHUSHA is seeking souls for eternal life, Satan is seeking souls for eternal death.

Even with all the complexities in the spiritual legal system, one thing is for certain. Alahym is righteous. The depths of those words carry deep truth. YAHUSHA is so righteous, that even when the enemy petitions the court of heaven, to steal, kill, or destroy someone or something if it is according to the Word, YAHUSHA will grant it. Sin tips the scale in favor of the prosecutor. Let's take it a step further. Sin not only opens the door to a person's physical body and life but can open generational doorways. A door that gives demons the legal right to oppress future generations. Doorways are things like engaging in fornication, masturbation, perversion (oral sex, bestiality, etc), pornography, unforgiveness, bitterness, carnality, fear, doubt, witchcraft, molestation, abuse, emotional wounds, soul ties, lustful thoughts and things of this nature.

Think about it like this. In a court of law, oaths, agreements, contracts, and covenants are binding. It's an agreement between two parties. Whatever written in it stands, and the objectives must be upheld by both parties. If a person breaches a contract by not fulfilling the words written in it, they will be subject to judgment. The first party presents the oath, agreement, contract, or covenant. The second party then agrees or disagrees with the terms to be fulfilled. Shift to the spiritual world and the two parties which are YAHUAH and Satan. They both offer oaths, agreements, contracts, covenants which are sealed in blood. Words and deeds are pens. These pens sign contracts to life or death. For we know that "life and death are in the power of the tongue (Mash/Pro 18:21)." In Barashith 3:4-5 (Genesis) Satan offers an oath, agreement, contract, covenant to Hauuah (Eve). She 'ate the fruit' metaphorical, and signed on the dotted line. Then she gave the oath, contract, agreement, covenant to Adam, and he signed it as he 'ate the fruit.' Legally, they handed over the dominion of the earth to Satan (Yahu/John 14:30). Thus, by the law of YAHUAH, the dominion that was given to Adam in Barashith 1:26 (Genesis), is now Satan's, but only for short time.

Since the dominion of the earth is in the hands of Satan, things are in chaos. As Sons and Daughters of YAHUAH, we are against Satan and the chaos. The Righteous are vessels spreading the Kingdom of YAHUAH on earth, reprimanding darkness.

Master YAHUSHA said, "And I shall give you the keys of the reign of the heavens, and whatever you bind on earth shall be having been bound in the heavens, and whatever you loose on earth shall be having been loosened in the heavens (Matt 16:19)." Upon deeper inspection, we see that this is also a declaration which speaks of our authority. To bind means to forbid, prohibit, declare illicit or illegal. To loose means to unbind, set free, discharge undo, break up, and to declare unlawful. Now let's return to the spirit of Kalab (Caleb). When he saw the Anaq, he responded in complete trust of YAHUAH. When the people spoke in fear, "Kalab (Caleb) silenced the people..." He binds up their fears because it was opposite of what the Word previous told them. Anything in the universe that is contrary to the righteousness of the Word, is illegal. It is sin because it transgresses the law of YAHUAH. Once Kalab (Caleb) bond the people's fears, he loosed complete trust in Alahym, taking up authority they had been given.

These are the basic warfare principles, yet many people have overlooked them for centuries. I didn't know either until I went through spiritual boot camp. Ignorance of these principles has handicapped many people in spiritual battles. From personal trials brought on by sin, to generational curses, one thing is constant. To be free, you must first realize what is lawful and unlawful. You must realize you are enslaved, and how unlawful slavery is. "For a man is a slave to whatever has overcome him (2 Kapha/Peter 2:19)." What enslaves all men? Sin! Only by the blood of YAHUSHA Messiah can you be redeemed from sin and death. An ever growing relationship with Alahym the Father will open a door for Him to give you His spirit and teach you His statutes and commandments. This will provide you with an opportunity to possess the authority that you have been given. Hazon 14:12 (Revelation) said it best, "Here is the endurance of the set-apart ones, those guarding the commands of Alahym and the belief of YAHUSHA." Are you ready for war?

PRAYER AGAINST GENERATIONAL CURSES

I submit myself to Alahym and am 100% dedicated and committed to YAHUSHA Messiah. I have faith and trust in Him to lead and shepherd my life. For I have lost my life and gained abundant and eternal life in Him. I am not my own, for I was brought with a price. In Him, I have redemption through His blood. I've received the forgiveness of my trespasses, according to the riches of His favor. I am His workmanship, created in Messiah YAHUSHA unto good works, which Alahym the Father prepared beforehand that I should walk in them. Thus, I obey the voice of YAHUAH my Alahym, to guard to do all His commands which He commands me.

Alahym the Father through Master YAHUSHA has redeemed me from the curse of the law. In His Name and authority, I break all generational curses of pride, lust, perversion, rebellion, witchcraft, idolatry, poverty, rejection, fear, confusion, addiction, death, and destruction in the Name of YAHUSHA, by His blood.

I command all generational spirits that came into my life during conception, in the womb, in the birth canal, and through the umbilical cord to come out in the Name of YAHUSHA. I take authority over (name the spirits) in the Name of YAHUSHA my Master, and according to Luke 10:19. I bind (name the spirits) and declare you trespassers, you may not function here. I command you to leave in the Name of YAHUSHA.

I break all spoken curses and negative words that I have spoken over my life in the Name of YAHUSHA. I break all spoken curses and negative words spoken over my life by others, including those in authority, in the Name of YAHUSHA. I command all ancestral spirits of Freemasonry, idolatry, witchcraft, false religion, lust, and perversion to come out of my life in the Name of YAHUSHA. I command all hereditary spirits of lust, rejection, fear, sickness, infirmity, disease, anger, hatred, confusion, failure, and poverty to come out of my life, in the Name of YAHUSHA. I break the legal rights of all generational spirits operating behind a curse in the Name of YAHUSHA. You spirits have no legal right to operate in my life. I bind and rebuke all familiar spirits and spirit guides that would try to operate in my life from my ancestors in the Name of YAHUSHA. I renounce all false beliefs and philosophies inherited by my ancestors in the Name of YAHUSHA. Any spiritual doorways that I have opened by sin, that is breaking the Turah (Torah) in any location, that has opened doorways for Satan to operate freely, I repent and turn from. I wash my garments in the Blood of the Lamb. I break all curses of sickness and disease and command all inherited sickness to leave my body in the Name of YAHUSHA. Through YAHUSHA, my family is blessed. I renounce all pride inherited from my ancestors in the Name of YAHUSHA. I break all oaths, vows, and pacts made with the devil by my ancestors in the Name of YAHUSHA. I break all curses by agents of Satan spoken against my life in secret in the Name of YAHUSHA. I break all written curses that would affect my life or my children's lives, in the Name of YAHUSHA. I break time-released curses that would try to activate in my life or my children's lives as we grow older, in the Name of YAHUSHA. I break every curse Balaam hired against my life in the Name of YAHUSHA. Alahym YAHUAH turns every curse spoken against my life into a blessing. I break all generational rebellion was would cause me to resist the Ruach Ha Qdush (Set-Apart Spirit). I break all curses of death spoken by people in authority over my family and over your nation in the Name of YAHUSHA. YAHUAH baruch (bless) me to be a baruch, and guard me; YAHUAH make Your face shine upon me, and show favour to me; YAHUAH lift up Your face upon me, and give me shalum (peace)." Heavenly Father, please hear the prayer of Your servant! In the authority and Name of YAHUSHA. Aman. Praise YAHUAH!

THE PROMISED LAND

If you have applied some of the tools and lessons in *The Wilderness*, then you've made it to the edge of the Promised Land! A praise session to YAHUAH is due. The Promised Land in *The Wilderness*, wasn't a location. Neither was it the possession of tangible things. No, it's so much more. It's power and wisdom from on high. Transformation power through Alahym's Ruach Ha Qdush (Set-Apart Spirit). May you repent and call upon His name and receive His Spirit. That you may become a new creature, through the Messiah. Thank the Father for sending His son. To die that day, and rise with all power and might. Redeeming power from sin and death. Mmmm. Power strong enough to redeem you from any sin. I can remember times were I thought I would never be free from sin. It was a lie. There is life and freedom in YAHUSHA, and I didn't just read that in the Book. Free from sin and all that weighs us down. He made me a new tree, and the old one is gone.

Alahym took me through the fire for you. You've been through the fire for others. Pay it forward. This is what the wilderness was intended for. For purging, to prepare you for the Promised Land. You can't take those habits or secret sins into this land flowing with milk and honey. You will destroy everything. Look at it like this. Will Alahym invite sinners to that Kingdom City, the New Yarushalayim (Jerusalem)? You already know the answer to that one. Then why think, He will let us go to the next level in our being and purpose without being whole? I was naive to once believe that. You may look at people in the world, who front as if their in their "Promised Land," but there's only one problem. They cheated and left their soul in the wilderness. Not so with you. I believe Alahym arranges supernatural appoints, this is why you are reading this book. I have faith that you will go through the process and not cut corners. Becoming all the person YAHUAH created you to be.

As I write you, I'm entering my own Promised Land. Full of giants who look like grasshoppers, and all sorts of challenges, which I have already won, because YAHUAH is with me. However, let's get one thing straight. Though you make it to the Promised Land, the place where you become whole in character, and your dreams and heavenly purpose begin to manifest, does not mean the battle is over. In fact, it has just begun. It is not time to rest, but is a time of adventure and war. It reminds me of what happened after Mushah (Moses) died, and Yashra'al (Israel) was about to enter the Promised Land.

It was such a blessing and pleasure to share these things with you. I wanted to end with one of my favorite scripture passages. These verses put the finishing touches on the journey through *The Wilderness*. "And it came to be, after the death of Mushah (Moses) the servant of YAHUAH, that YAHUAH spoke to Yahusha (Joshua) son of Nun, the assistant of Mushah (Moses), saying, "Mushah (Moses) My servant is dead, so now, arise, pass over this Yardan (Jordan), you and all this people, to the land which I am giving to them, to the children of Yashra'al (Israel). "Every place on which the sole of your foot treads I have given you, as I spoke to Mushah (Moses). "No man is going to stand before you all the days of your life. As I was with Mushah (Moses), so I am with you. I do not fail you nor forsake you. "Be strong and courageous, for you are to let this people inherit the land which I swore to their fathers to give them. "Only be strong and very courageous, to guard to do according to all the Turah (Torah) which Mushah (Moses) My servant commanded you. Do not turn from it right or left, so that you act wisely wherever you go. "Do not let this Book of the Turah (Torah) depart from your mouth, but you shall meditate on it day and night, so that you guard to do according to all that is written in it. For then you shall make your way prosperous, and act wisely. "Have I not commanded you? Be strong and courageous. Do not be afraid, nor be discouraged, for YAHUAH your Alahym is with you wherever you go (Yahu/Josh 1:1-3, 5-9)."

Notes

OPEN LETTERS

1. Star-Spangled Bigotry: The Hidden Racist History of the National Anthem
   https://www.theroot.com/star-spangled-bigotry-the-hidden-racist-history-of-the-1790855893
2. San Miguel de Guadalupe
   https://en.wikipedia.org/wiki/San_Miguel_de_Guadalupe
3. John Hawkins
   https://www.rmg.co.uk/discover/explore/sir-john-hawkins
4. Queen Elizabeth
   https://books.google.com/books?isbn=1317432452
5. The Good Ship Jesus
   https://en.wikipedia.org/wiki/Jesus_of_L%C3%BCbeck
6. Mass Incarceration Mystery
   https://www.washingtonpost.com/news/wonk/wp/2017/12/15/a-mass-incarceration-mystery/?noredirect=on

LIFE LESSONS

7. WHO Statistics
   https://www.usnews.com/news/best-countries/articles/2016-09-14/the-10-most-depressed-countries
8. Science of Happiness
   https://greatergood.berkeley.edu/article/item/the_science_of_happiness_coming_soon_to_a_theater_near_you
9. Lifestyle Definition
   http://www.businessdictionary.com/definition/lifestyle.html

REVELATIONS

10. Copernican Heliocentrism
    https://en.wikipedia.org/wiki/Copernican_heliocentrism

NOTES

11. Center of the universe
    http://www.reach-unlimited.com/p/1039043492/planck-satellite-data-confirm-earth-may-be-the-center-of-universe

12. Buttonwood Agreement
    https://www.theroot.com/how-slave-labor-made-new-york-1790895122

13. Wall Street
    https://en.wikipedia.org/wiki/Wall_Street

14. Average Household Income
    https://www.thebalance.com/what-is-average-income-in-usa-family-household-history-3306189

15. Mk-Ultra
    https://en.wikipedia.org/wiki/Project_MKUltra

16. Operation Paperclip
    https://en.wikipedia.org/wiki/Operation_Paperclip

17. DNA Cells
    https://www.smithsonianmag.com/smart-news/there-are-372-trillion-cells-in-your-body-4941473/
    http://www.wowreally.blog/2006/11/your-dna-would-reach-moon.html

18. Repair enzymes
    https://www.sciencedirect.com/topics/medicine-and-dentistry/repair-enzyme
    https://www6.slac.stanford.edu/news/2017-12-04-research-zooms-enzyme-repairs-dna-damage-uv-rays.aspx

19. Juno Moneta
    https://en.wikipedia.org/wiki/Moneta

Made in the USA
San Bernardino, CA
18 December 2018